John Wanamaker

KING OF
MERCHANTS

John Wanamaker

KING OF
MERCHANTS

to Bob and Barbara Straton
Friends for many, many years
Hope you enjoy the book,

William Allen Zulker

Bill Zulker
Sept. 1993

EAGLECREST PRESS
P.O. Box 9, Wayne, Pa. 19087

John Wanamaker: King of Merchants

Copyright 1993 by William Allen Zulker

For information, address:
      Eaglecrest Press
      P.O. Box 9
      Wayne, Pa. 19087

ISBN 0-9636284-1-0

Library of Congress Catalog Card Number: 93-90581

Printed in the United States of America

Hardcover 0-9636284-0-2

To Isabel

My wife of more than forty years

Mother of three of the world's loveliest daughters

Grandmother of eight of the world's busiest, non-stop kids

Table of Contents

Foreword

From the Sociological Imagination

JOHN WANAMAKER REPRESENTS AN AMERICA THAT WAS. A study of his life is a call to greatness that we hope and pray will come to America again. He was the sort of man who inspired the Horatio Alger novels, and his character was of the kind that led the French journalist, Alexis de Tocqueville, to believe that Americans were the best human beings that the planet had to offer.

As I read this biography by William Allen Zulker, I realized that John Wanamaker was almost what we sociologists call an "ideal type." In so many ways I found him to be a hypothetical construct rather than an existential reality. He jumped out of the pages of this book and presented himself to me as an incarnation of some of the most basic categories of my discipline.

I

THE FIRST OF THESE IDEAL TYPES which Wanamaker represented to me was that of the True Calvinist. I thought to myself that Max Weber, the German sociologist who wrote the classic essay, "The Protestant Ethic and the Spirit of Capitalism," could have used Wanamaker as a manifestation of that intensely hard-working Christian whose drive for success, he believed, came not from a love for money, but from deep-rooted spiritual convictions.

It was Weber's thesis that Calvinistic protestantism tends to produce an "ideal type," whose industry in the marketplace does not grow out of that psychological sickness which typifies so many workaholics, but instead comes out of a deep conviction that being a merchant is a divine calling. According to Weber, the Calvinists believe that spiritual salvation has nothing to do with a person's virtue or individualistic decisions but is dependent upon Divine Election. Thus, says Weber, for the Calvinist, all good works flow from the *gratitude* a person feels because of being pre-destined before the foundation of the earth to be part of the family of God. The zeal generated from this gratitude, Weber contended, was what provided the "holy" drivenness that made men like Wanamaker the suc-cessful engines which pulled America into modern capitalism.

The spiritually generated drivenness that Weber saw in the ideal-type Calvinist was evident throughout Wanamaker's life. Furthermore, Wanamaker brought this same drivenness to both his commercial and his spiritual ventures. The connectedness between the two was so obvious in this man that it often was hard to discern whether he was a merchant or a preacher. On the one hand, he founded the largest department store in the world. But on the other hand, he established the largest Sunday School in the world.

Wanamaker's inventiveness in business led to his providing such things as complete medical coverage for his tens of thousands of employ-ees, education for those youngsters who were in his employ because eco-nomic necessity had required that they drop out of school and support their families, two-week vacations for his workers at a time when such things were unheard of, the equivalent of a company credit union for those who would not have been considered by banks, and a host of cultur-al activities for common folk who otherwise never would have tasted of the fine arts.

His creative entrepreneurial spirit in the realm of religious faith made Wanamaker a prime mover in bringing the Y.M.C.A. to cities around the world. He did this at a time when the word "Christian" was the *raison d'etre* of that organization. He was a leading organizer of the famous Dwight L. Moody revival meetings that impacted his beloved Philadelphia, and he planted new churches throughout the Delaware Valley region that he always considered to be his home.

With Wanamaker there was never a clear delineation between the sphere of faith and the sphere of business. Consequently, it is no wonder that he was accused of using his religion to further his business and, con-trariwise, was accused of using his business to further his religion. It is impossible to determine where the one ended and the other began. All of Wanamaker's activities flowed together and seemed to speak of his thankfulness to God for the salvation that seemed to him so rich and free and which he always felt he did not deserve.

John Wanamaker was a Presbyterian, and he embraced that denomination's teachings about stewardship. He made generous giving to the cause of his God the essence of his life. He was a "this world" Christian in the sense that he believed that the "cultural mandate," as John Calvin called it, required him to be an agent of change, committed to using all of his assets and gifts to transform society into something that looked more like the Kingdom of God.

Had Weber known John Wanamaker, he would have pointed to him as the "ideal type" of person who gave expression to the religiosity that would make America into a commercial success.

II

THE SECOND SOCIOLOGICAL CONCEPT that John Wanamaker brought to my mind as I read Zulker's book was the "Inner-Directed Person," described by David Reisman, the Harvard sociologist.

Reisman, in his famous book, *The Lonely Crowd*, constructed an image of a person who has deeply rooted principles that guide his or her life and who lives according to those principles regardless of what others might think or say. Such an inner directed person, according to Reisman, is one who knows what is right and does it without considering social or economic consequences.

An inner-directed man like John Wanamaker could be hard to get along with in everyday life. He was a man who did not understand the meaning of compromise.

Wanamaker dominated the entire social landscape of a city where, a hundred years earlier, some other inner-directed men gave birth to a nation. In business, he made the concept of a "fixed price" in his stores a hallmark of his honesty. When he said that he was selling his goods at the best price possible, he meant it, and there was nothing to talk about. Bargaining requires pretending and maybe even lying. What goes on in many of the exotic bazaars of other countries requires that people "put on" that they are selling and buying at the best possible price, when such is not the case. Hucksters tell customers that they are making final offers that really are not final at all. Such deceptive game playing could not be part of the style of this inner-directed merchant. Wanamaker's principled dealings with people required that from the beginning of each transaction, the prices that he fixed on his goods as being final were final indeed. The prices he said were "the best" in town were exactly that.

It is no wonder that Wanamaker was a poor politician. Politics is a science of compromise, and an inner-directed person has not a clue as to how to play the game. Wanamaker ran unsuccessfully for the U.S.Senate and later tried to become Governor of his state. But he just did not have what it takes to live in an arena where "you have to go along, if you want to get along." Within politics, he was a naive virgin in a land of whores. The political machines run by cigar-smoking cronies who cut deals in back rooms had no place for "Pious John," as they called him. They chewed him up and spit him out.

Wanamaker never really got a handle on what was going on in politics. He thought that all you needed to do was to be honest, bright and hard-working. He thought that virtue made for winners on election day. Too often such principled inner-directed people can find no place in "cynic land" where "dirty tricks" seem to be the instruments of successful campaigns.

Wanamaker did become Postmaster General of the United States of America. But that cabinet post did not take political sophistication. The requirements to be a great Postmaster General were brilliant organizational skills, marketing innovations, the ability to manage people, and precision in bookkeeping. Wanamaker had all of those traits. Like most inner-directed people, he had no trouble with a clearly defined job that required forthrightness and honesty. But when it came to being in the halls of Congress, one might ask, "What would a nice guy like him be doing in a place like that?"

III

FINALLY, I CALL YOUR ATTENTION to Robert Bellah's best selling book, *Habits of the Heart*. Bellah tells us about "the true citizen," that well-balanced person who always has a deep commitment to civic duty.

According to Bellah, the sickness that pervades our contemporary social scene, and will destroy it if we do not find a cure for it, is "effective individualism." He tells us that today's society is preoccupied with seeking a "self actualization" that will deliver emotional fulfillment.

When American mothers are asked what they want their children to become when they grow up, they answer, "Happy!" Indeed, "the pursuit of happiness" has become for us Americans not simply a right but an obligation. And it is this commitment to egoistic gratification to which Bellah refers when he describes us as highly unbalanced in the direction of "effective individualism." He tells us that we have lost the countervailing effects that come from a sense of obligation to others. For most people today, it seems as though self-centered happiness is all that matters. In our world, husbands and wives walk out, both on each other and on their children, if family duties interfere with individualistic fulfillment. Obligations in business are now often held lightly, and contracts, even if they are written, are easily broken if individuals do not find them to their likening. The laws of the land are, as Shakespeare had Hamlet say, "More honored in the breech than in the observance."

Doing what we are supposed to do is something that, for the most part, is done these days only if the doing is convenient to our personal happiness. We have become a sensate people, and living up to one's duty belongs to another era. It belongs to John Wanamaker's era. He was one of those who embraced duty with a passion and made it into a creed. Wanamaker always did what duty required. He did it for his employees. He did for his city. And when his nation went to war, he volunteered to go and do it for America. He even promised salaries for time in military service to any of his employees who would go and do their patriotic duty. He trained his young employees to be "cadets" and taught them how to march and take orders, for whether at home, at work, or at play, those associated with him were expected to behave like dutiful soldiers.

Wanamaker's religion was duty bound, too. We can almost hear him singing, "Onward, Christian soldiers, Marching as to war, With the cross of Jesus, Going on before." He did what the Bible told him to do. There was no hint of "situational ethics" in his character. He may have been a warm person, but he was unwavering and firm in his commitment to duty. He required this same high commitment to duty of his own kin. He was a faithful father, husband and citizen. "There was no shadow of turning" in his personality.

On the east side of the Philadelphia City Hall stands a statue of our hero. He is positioned in a purposeful stance. You cannot look at this likeness without sensing that this was a man going someplace and he was certain as to where it was.

The words inscribed beneath the statue are his name and the simple word "Citizen." In this age when we are not quite sure what the word "citizen" means, we need to know more about John Wanamaker.

ANTHONY (TONY) CAMPOLO, PH.D
Sociologist
Professor-at-Large
Eastern College
St. Davids, Pennsylvania

Preface

WHEN I BEGAN to review the vast collection of the Wanamaker papers—stored in more than 100 large cartons—I had no intentions of writing a book. I was interested only in knowing more about John Wanamaker for my own enjoyment. As I discovered the scope of his involvement in business, politics, religious organizations, the educational world and life in general, it became imperative to me for others to hear the story, too. Almost five years later this book has become a reality.

William Allen Zulker

ACKNOWLEDGMENTS

THOUGH A BOOK MAY BE THE INSPIRATION of a single mind it is the product of many people combining their talents.

Of the many people who have helped me, I am indeed grateful to my wife, Isabel, and our three daughters, Barbara Zulker, Beverly Vesper and Beth Mellon who were patient, understanding and supportive at all times. Each contributed in her own way, assisting me in conducting voluminous correspondence, organizing files, proofreading my manuscript, and typing mailing lists. Above all they provided encouragement when the thrill of writing, at times, became laborious. The main task of preparing the manuscript was assumed by Beth who spent many hours and days at the computer translating my scribblings into intelligible sentences. Her untiring, easy-going manner and attention to minute details—despite her professional employment and family of six—kept the project afloat. Without her help the book would not have happened.

Dr. Anthony Campolo, world-renowned sociologist, has greatly honored me by writing the foreword.

I am also indebted to Linda Stanley, Vice President of the Historical Society of Pennsylvania, who initially opened the Wanamaker collection to me, and Louise Jones, Acting Curator of Manuscripts, who have given me unhindered access to the collection. Others who have provided information and assistance are John R. Wanamaker, Kenneth A. Hammonds, George Ambrose, Alice Gilliam, Nelson Buechner, Peter van der Stek, Mary Alice Hennessey, Sue Morgan, Al Goessler, Fred Yost, Charles Davies, John Leone, Myra Schutz, Willard Wellman, John Michael Powell, Bill Brey, Helen Gemmill, Eugenia Meade, Herb Collins, Jim Bruns, Herb Erschowitz, John Platt, Milt Kennin, Donald McDonald, Howard Schmertz, Julie Ericksen, Cliff R. Gillam, Jr., Jan Heppe, Raymond Holstein, Doug Elliott, Donna Taylor, Nancy Montgomery, Florence Williams, and Mary Moore.

Permission to use and reproduce photographs and other materials in their control has been granted by the Historical Society of Pennsylvania, *The Farm Journal*, HarperCollins Publishers, Fleming H. Revell-Baker Book House, The MacMillan Publishing Co., Julian and Pamela Beck of Washington Conn., Joey and Toby Tannenbaum of Toronto, Canada, The Grand Lodge of Pennsylvania, Henry Baecker, Florence Williams, Myra Schutz, Widener University and Mr. John Rodman Wanamaker, great-grandson of the Founder and former Chairman of the Board of John Wanamaker.

The manuscript was edited by Marti Meyer who allowed me to maintain my own style of writing, but protected me from unnecessary pitfalls. Stephanie Young, with her deft hand and pen, designed the book and cover—enhancing my vision many-fold—and maintained oversight of the total production of the book. Jim Mellon and Tim Scott-Spencer Studios were responsible for photographic reproductions.

WAZ

PHOTOCREDITS

Most of the illustrations in this book have been reproduced from the Wanamaker Collection at the Historical Society of Pennsylvania, Philadelphia, Pa., noted HSP. Permission has been granted by both the Society and Mr. John R. Wanamaker.

Introduction

THE NAME OF JOHN WANAMAKER was a household word for many years. Founder of the department store, pioneer in the mercantile business, public servant, church builder and humanitarian, Wanamaker combined the principles of his deep religious faith with the practices of his dry goods and clothing business. Even though he headed the largest clothing establishment in America at one time with more than 12,000 employees, Wanamaker did not let success go to his head. He never veered from his desire to put other people first.

Some lives speak more eloquently than words. Such was the life of Wanamaker. He treated customers as those who had "rights," a new concept in his day. He spoke of "mutuality," meaning that there was a benefit for both the proprietor and the customer when business was managed properly. He gave his employees free medical treatment, educational courses, recreational facilities, pensions, and profit-sharing plans. He built relationships with manufacturers, tradespeople, employees and buyers on the foundation of truth, honesty, fairness and decency.

He said, "I always believed there was a better way to run a business than just to make money." But money he made, and lots of it, leaving an estate valued at $35 million in 1922.

Self in the present age seems preeminent. The me-first philosophy is not only embraced by many, but also widely encouraged. Is there another way to live? Wanamaker, despite heavy odds against him, firmly took his stand and boldly demonstrated that there is. His life was an eighty-four-year commentary, teaching by example, not by injunction.

This book, *John Wanamaker: King of Merchants*, presents a capsule of the life of this remarkable man. Much of his story is told through his personal letters to family and friends, his speeches, store editorials and other writings.

William Allen Zulker
June 1993

A Young Lad Keeps His Vow

ON THE DAY BEFORE CHRISTMAS 1850, a twelve-year-old boy went looking for a present for his mother.

Upon entering a jewelry store, he made his selection. As the storekeeper was wrapping the purchase, the young lad saw something else he liked better.

Telling the man he had changed his mind, the boy was told, "It's too late, you've already bought this."

As he left the store with his package he made a vow, "Some day I'll own a store and I'll treat my customers kindly and fairly." [1]

The boy kept his vow as he began his first business in 1861 at Sixth and High Streets in Philadelphia. With the basic principle of customer satisfaction, the store that bore his name, John Wanamaker, soon became the largest retail store in America.

This book tells more of the story of the incomparable John Wanamaker.

John Wanamaker,
twenty-five years old

Wanamaker's Grand Depot Lives On

OVER ONE HUNDRED YEARS AGO on May 6, 1876, John Wanamaker opened the doors of his new store, The Grand Depot, at Thirteenth and Market Streets, the present location of the flagship store in the heart of Philadelphia.

He called it "Depot" because the building had been a freight station of the Pennsylvania Railroad from 1853 to 1874. By today's standards it would hardly be described as "grand," for it was nothing more than an ungainly wooden train-shed covering two acres. Inside this one-story structure hung large paper clover-leaves upon which were printed the "four cardinal principles" of the Wanamaker business: One Price For All; Full Guarantee; Cash Payment; and Cash Returned. Announcing and practicing these rights for the customer was basic to the store's success.

Wanamaker then filled the two-acre building with merchandise and 129 counters for his customers' convenience. Transformed, The Grand Depot became the store that covered more ground space than any other in the nation.

Immediately the Grand Depot became a sight-seeing attraction for visitors who had come to Philadelphia for the United States Centennial in Fairmount Park. Seven-and-a-half million of them came. Almost a million had never been in the City of Brotherly Love before, and many found their way to the Grand Depot. With pennants flying from flag poles at the four corners of the building the Grand Depot appeared to be an annex to the Centennial itself.

Fifteen years earlier, Wanamaker had entered the clothing business at Sixth and High (now Market) Streets. He was touted as being too young, at twenty-two, to compete with the older and experienced clothiers of the day. Moreover, 1861 was the worst time in many years for anything new to be undertaken in the commercial world as the country faced the possibility of internal war. Indeed just ninety-four hours after the start of business, the Confederates fired upon Fort Sumter, opening a new era in the history of the young nation. Yet Wanamaker and Nathan Brown, his brother-in-law and partner, were not discouraged by adversity.

The location Wanamaker had chosen for his first store was prime for business. Commercial activities stretched from the Delaware River up High Street to a little beyond Eighth Street. Oak Hall, as he called the new store, was convenient for all.

The site of his venture was also historic. The home of Philadelphia's famous financier, Robert Morris, originally stood on this corner, and George Washington had resided next door when Philadelphia was the United States' Capitol. It seems almost true to form that the founding of what would become America's foremost department store also began here. Today, the Liberty Bell is housed just a few feet away from where the first John Wanamaker store opened its doors.

Similarly, the site of his new store, The Grand Depot, at Thirteenth and Market was also historic. Philadelphia's Central High School stood on this spot from 1838 until the lot was purchased by the Pennsylvania Railroad. Adjoining the site was the oldest arsenal in the country, built in 1785. Across the way stood the United States Mint, the birthplace of American photography. Here Joseph Saxton took his picture of Central High, the oldest known American photograph still in existence. John Wanamaker loved history. He loved making it too.

Before Wanamaker entered the clothing business, he served as the first paid secretary of the Y.M.C.A. Though introduced to the Board of Directors as "the boy with the funny name that no one has ever heard of," by the end of the century he had become Philadelphia's most prominent citizen. Today, more than seventy years after his death in 1922, his signature, emblazoned upon the entrances of fifteen stores and upon millions of shopping bags and boxes, remains so well recognized that many people think that John Wanamaker is still living.

After several attempts to restructure The Grand Depot to meet the ever-increasing volume of business, Wanamaker started constructing the present granite and steel twelve-story building. It took a period of nine years to build the largest retail store in the world. On December 30, 1911, President William Howard Taft dedicated the building while 25,000 people celebrated together in the Grand Court.

Never lost for timely and enduring words, Wanamaker placed the capstone on the roof of the new building and stated, "Let those who follow me, build with the plumb of Honor, the level of Truth, and the square of Integrity, Education, Courtesy and Mutuality."

Bird's-eye view of the interior of the Wanamaker Grand Depot (1877)

A Child Is Born

JULY 11, 1838 SEEMED TO BE JUST ANOTHER DAY in the life of most Philadelphians. But for Nelson Wanamaker, a brickmaker, and his wife, Elizabeth DeShong Kochersperger, it was the day of birth of their first child—a son. They named him John after his paternal grandfather who was a farmer, builder, abolitionist, and part-time country preacher with a pioneer spirit. Some of these same characteristics later surfaced in the newborn grandchild.

The population of Philadelphia—less than 200,000—was concentrated in a small area between the Delaware and Schuylkill Rivers and South and Vine Streets. The land beyond was more country than the suburbs known today. The small Wanamaker brick-yard and two-story farm house at Buck Road and Long Lane—near Gray's Ferry—was surrounded by farms, swamps and ponds where the children swam and fished.

As the young boy grew, soon joined by three brothers and three sisters, he helped his father in the backyard by turning bricks to dry in the sun. There was no school for him to attend until he was nine years of age. Then the city bought a building, the Landreth house, and his grandfather was elected the first president of the local school board. Sundays, of course, were spent in church and Sunday School where both John's father and grandfather were teachers. Three years later his education came to an end as the family moved away from Philadelphia.

INDIANA BOUND

WITH THE EXPANSION OF THE RAILROADS, the accompanying problems of tramps and rowdy gangs in their neighborhood and the development of larger brick yards competing for business, John's parents were attracted to the simple frontier life of Indiana. Relatives reported Indiana to be like "a land of milk and honey" with unlimited possibilities and a safe place for a growing family.

Selling the brickyard, Nelson and his wife packed up their family and household possessions and moved to Leesburg, a journey enjoyed by the boys, but one that almost took the life of Elizabeth and the new baby. Nearby was an Indian reservation with real-life Indians living in wigwams and huts carrying on their own traditions. Life here was a delightful and unforgettable experience for twelve-year-old John.

But after a hard winter, unlike anything they had experienced in Philadelphia, John's parents decided to return to Philadelphia where they would be close to Elizabeth's family. Leaving his grandfather in Indiana was a difficult move for John whose love and admiration never diminished for the man for whom he was named.

BACK TO PHILADELPHIA

UPON THE FAMILY'S RETURN to the City of Brotherly Love, John sought employment away from the brickyards. His first job at Troutman and Hayes' bookstore on Market Street near Fifth was as an errand boy for $1.25 a week. The store was a long walk from home, but he was glad to earn some money to help pay the family's bills. A year later he found a better job paying twice the salary at Barclay Lippincott's clothing store. This was his introduction to the trade that later became his life's work.

Just up the street, Colonel Bennett's Tower Hall seemed even more attractive to John with its exciting advertisements and displays. This clothing establishment occupied a much larger building and had the best reputation in the city, an important factor to Wanamaker even in his youth. As soon as he could, John applied to Bennett's.

At a beginning weekly salary of $6.00, the young man was employed by Bennett to do the most menial tasks until he learned the stock. Promoted to salesman, he soon became manager of the men's furnishing department even though he was but nineteen. It was obvious that the young lad was on the move to better things with a momentum that was irrepressible.

Just when John seemed to have decided to become a merchant, his health broke. His physician advised him to stop working, leave the area and seek a complete change and rest. With meager savings he left

Philadelphia to travel, first to Chicago and then on to Minnesota. He described the journey of over 3,500 miles as "wandering among mountains and prairies, up and down rivers and streams."

It was also a time of personal reflection upon religion and his values in life. In a letter written while he was traveling he said:

> My health has been in a great measure restored and shall, the Lord willing, soon return. I hope with renewed energy to engage in the service of the Lord. In conclusion I ask an interest in your prayers that I may be a humble and faithful child of God. [1]

It is particularly surprising to note that when he returned home, he did not resume employment in the clothing business with Colonel Bennett or another similar establishment. Rather, he accepted a salaried position as Secretary of the Philadelphia Y.M.C.A.

Birthplace of John Wanamaker,
Philadelphia, Pa.

The Y.M.C.A. Secretary, President and Benefactor

A GROUP OF PHILADELPHIA AREA CLERGYMEN, encouraged by George H. Smith, a young and prominent businessman, met in 1854 at Jaynes Hall on Sansom Street. They organized themselves as the Philadelphia Young Men's Christian Association, with Smith as their president.

Originally founded in England in 1844 by George Williams, a merchant, the Y.M.C.A. spread to America and other major countries.

One of the first endeavors of the Philadelphia group was the sponsorship of Sunday evening Bible classes throughout the city. The group also wanted to strengthen and improve existing Sunday Schools and to begin others. Their stated goal was "to reach the many thousands of neglected children and youth not likely to be brought under any moral influence by other means." Evangelism was the group's primary focus.

John Wanamaker, age twenty, was employed to provide leadership for the fledgling organization in 1858. Though he had been actively engaged as a volunteer teacher in the First Independent Church with Rev. John Chambers as his pastor, he was introduced to the Y.M.C.A. Board by Mr. Smith as "the young man with the funny name that no one has ever heard of." As the first, paid, full-time secretary (general director), Wanamaker was charged to set up training programs and coordinate all activities of the association.

Wanamaker was given an annual salary of $1000, a large sum in those days. By the end of his first year, though, he had proved his worth: the organization grew from its original membership of fifty-seven men to more than two thousand. He had also supervised the distribution of hundreds of New Testaments, enlisted and trained more than forty young men as Sunday School teachers and secured many pledges of total abstinence, an endeavor he kept up throughout his lifetime.

It was said of Wanamaker that "he disliked tobacco but he hated alcohol." He regularly distributed "Abstinence Pledge" cards, which he had printed with the picture of Abraham Lincoln, claiming that Lincoln had written the pledge.

The city was ripe for any religious effort in the 1850s due to a continuing influx of young men who had left their country homes to find adventure, employment and success in the growing city. The city was a strange world for them, where, without home guidance or family restraints and faced with anonymity, they soon became lonely. Moral decay and despair followed.

Many churches saw the problem but were ineffective in reaching the newcomers, for religion, as practiced in the church, seemed unattractive to them. The Y.M.C.A. worked as a para-church organization in bringing young men together and providing moral and spiritual direction through a great variety of activities. Without apology to anyone, the Y.M.C.A. centered itself upon Biblical teaching and made a conscious evangelistic effort "to bring the youth to faith in Jesus Christ."

Despite the indifference of some pastors and churches and direct opposition from others, young Wanamaker and the other leaders of the Y.M.C.A. labored diligently. He demonstrated that their methods were different but their goals were the same. The religious revival that had recently swept the city was perpetuated by their efforts. The Y.M.C.A. sponsored numerous tent meetings every day of the week during the summer with the exception of Sunday mornings and Wednesday evenings, so as not to conflict with regular church services.

Wanamaker, with great delight and satisfaction, employed the superintendent of the Y.M.C.A. tent, giving detailed instructions regarding the number of meetings to be held, the hours of each, care of the tent, selection of preachers, records to be kept and the disposition of the money received in the offerings.

SETTING THE EXAMPLE

THROUGHOUT HIS LIFE, Wanamaker never asked others to do something that he himself had not done or was not willing to do. Like a captain, he was always with his troops. It is not surprising, then, to learn that during his first year as the Y.M.C.A. secretary, he founded the Sunday School which he named Bethany. He started with just twenty-seven students in a second-floor room over a cobbler's shop, and he set an example of what one person can do to share his faith with others.

For three years, he continued his employment with the Y.M.C.A. and learned a great deal about leadership. Reflecting Wanamaker's ability to organize and motivate others, the Philadelphia Y.M.C.A. became a model for other cities as the organization began to spread.

In 1860, while attending the National Convention of the Y.M.C.A. in New Orleans, Louisiana, Wanamaker seems to have decided to resign his employment with the organization, though his support for its work continued throughout his life. When he returned to Philadelphia, he married Mary Ann Brown and in the following year started his clothing business, Oak Hall.

When the Civil War began, he and several other Y.M.C.A. leaders met in New York to form the Christian Commission for the Army and Navy, endeavoring to promote both the temporal and spiritual welfare of military personnel. Appointed Secretary of the new organization, Wanamaker secured the approval of President Lincoln and aided in the enlistment of over 5,000 volunteers. He also helped to raise more than six million dollars to provide supplies for the wounded and returning veterans of battle.

In 1869, despite the responsibilities of managing the store alone after the death of his partner Nathan Brown, starting a second store on Chestnut Street and devoting much needed leadership to the rapidly growing Bethany Sunday School, he nevertheless accepted the presidency of the Y.M.C.A. following the resignation of George Stuart. Immediately he organized nearly 300 open-air religious meetings throughout the city during the summer months.

He also made overtures to the "Negro" clergy of Philadelphia who reported that there were 32,000 negroes living in the city. In cooperation with them he rented a house on Lombard Street for the "Colored Branch" of the Y.M.C.A. and served as a member of the First Interracial Committee. Sometime later he personally subscribed $25,000 enabling them to purchase their own building.

Never losing interest in the significance of the organization and wanting to be involved in the spreading movement, he attended as many of the National Conventions as possible: New York City in 1861, Saratoga Springs in 1863, Buffalo in 1868, and London in 1871 where he first met the founder George Williams. Again in London in 1894 for the Fiftieth Anniversary of its founding, he was not only one of the speakers at

Young Men's Christian Association building, Madras, India,
presented by John Wanamaker

Windsor Castle on this memorable occasion, but had the honor of being presented to Queen Victoria who was there to knight Williams for his distinguished service.

Numbered among Wanamaker's numerous philanthropic deeds was a $30,000 gift in 1897 for a Y.M.C.A. building in Madras, India. During his personal visit five years later he found a center for Christian teaching begun by a former Philadelphia Y.M.C.A. general secretary whom he had known back home.

He also gave buildings in Calcutta, India; Seoul, Korea; Kyoto, Japan; and Peking, China. In addition, the year before he died, he contributed money for a Y.M.C.A. to be built in Russia.

John R. Mott, an influential Christian during the early part of this century and General Secretary of the International Y.M.C.A., wrote:

> Not long before his death, Mr. Wanamaker wrote me promising to provide another building for the Y.M.C.A., this time in Russia....He indicated he wanted this building to be regarded as given in memory of Sir George Williams. [1]

Mott also stated that Wanamaker had contributed well over $200,000 for Y.M.C.A. buildings around the world.

So strongly did Wanamaker believe in the work of the Y.M.C.A. as a form of Christian ministry and service that when he gave a building to the Salvation Army at Broad and Fairmount Streets in Philadelphia, the legal papers stated that if they failed to remain true to the Gospel and "changed their fundamental basis" in ministry, the title of the property was to be relinquished to the Y.M.C.A.

A letter dated December 10, 1900 expressed his sentiments regarding the importance of the Y.M.C.A.:

> I am able to say, from forty years involvement and careful observation of Christian Association work, that I do not know of any other one organization that fills the exact place in relation to young men, that the Christian Association does.
>
> It is thoroughly practical at every point and I do not know of any greater loss to Philadelphia that could arise than the removal of the Christian Associations as the healthful centre and wholesome director of the young life of the men of our city. [2]

The enormous influence that Wanamaker had upon the Y.M.C.A. for more than sixty years can hardly be measured. By openly expressing his own personal faith with others, conducting religious meetings in tents and churches, starting Sunday Schools, developing organizational procedures and policies imitated throughout the nation, personally financing buildings, and promoting interracial and international relationships of good will, he lifted the Y.M.C.A. from being a tiny gathering of a few dozen men into a world-wide organization of prominence and prestige.

An Acorn Is Planted

OAK HALL

1861 WAS NOT A GOOD YEAR IN AMERICA, much less the right time to begin a new business. The winds of war were increasing in intensity. It was apparent to most that the conflict between the states would develop into a conflagration of death, despair and destruction.

Established businessmen worried with diminishing optimism about the future. But twenty-two-year-old John Wanamaker, with a young bride and an infant son, could not delay his plan of many months nor deny his vision. Ideal times and favorable circumstances might never coalesce for pioneers, yet they forge ahead. That's what gives pioneers their name. So on April 8 at 6:30 a.m., Wanamaker and his brother-in-law, Nathan Brown, opened Oak Hall, a men's and boys' clothing store at Sixth and High Streets in Philadelphia. Just ninety-four hours later, the Confederate Army fired shots upon Fort Sumter in Charleston Harbor, beginning the tragic and shameful Civil War.

Pooling resources to start their business, Wanamaker and Brown each invested $2,000, recorded in the first cash book found among the Founder's papers. Their small store measured only 30' x 80' on the first floor of a six-story building and held a limited inventory. A.T. Stewart in New York provided them with woolen merchandise on credit for thirty days. In addition the store offered ready-made clothing purchased at low prices directly from a manufacturer.

At first, only a few customers entered their store, and sales on the first day amounted to only $24.67. The daily cash book shows a steady decrease of "cash on hand" in the weeks that followed. Expenditures exceeded income with $365.00 spent on store fixtures, $1.00 for a receipt book, $1.50 for pattern paper, 25¢ for soap, 86¢ advertising for a cutter and 50¢ for supper for the two partners.

Not discouraged with the poor sales of the first day, they also secured contracts to manufacture military clothing and uniforms for guards at the nearby Customs House. Another expense, then, was paying the people who made the clothing. J.R. Houghton, a clothing cutter and friend of young John, received his first week's salary of $24.04, a large sum for that day and three times larger than the amount paid the second cutter. With the employment of additional tailors to make military uniforms, Wanamaker and Brown's Oak Hall was simultaneously becoming a manufacturer as well as a retail clothing store.

Their meager attempts at advertising began to pay off as curious readers came to test the accuracy and honesty of their ads. When they introduced special sales, a concept scorned by many merchants, their business began to increase, and the store expanded to a second floor next door. As each customer left the store, Wanamaker personally made it a point to inquire if they were satisfied with the service, a concern that contributed significantly to his later success.

At the end of the first year, total sales amounted to only $24,125.62. But by the end of the decade, annual sales had increased to "$2,085,528.55 with the store employing forty-three salesmen, seventy cutters and twenty clerks." The clothing firm of Wanamaker and Brown had become firmly established despite hardships.

When Nathan Brown died in 1868, Wanamaker was suddenly faced with full responsibility of the store, a circumstance that unquestionably forced him to demonstrate that his management and business capabilities equaled his limitless vision. However, Wanamaker never forgot the success that the two men shared during their first seven years, and the store continued to carry the name of his deceased partner as long as Oak Hall existed on Market Street.

Standing close by, with constant support and encouragement, Mary Wanamaker devoted herself to domestic concerns in order that her husband could fully conduct his growing business. On Sundays, both of them were immersed in the ministry of Bethany Chapel, which seemed to be an arsenal of faith, equipping them with courage for the week that followed.

The year after Nathan Brown's death, Wanamaker opened a second store at 818 Chestnut Street and began capitalizing upon his own name and growing reputation by calling the new store "John Wanamaker &

Oak Hall, Sixth and Market Streets, Philadelphia,
John Wanamaker and Nathan Brown, partners

Co." While the new store appealed to a higher class clientele, Wanamaker nevertheless continued to emphasize the principles first announced at Oak Hall in 1865: "One price and goods returnable."

Shortly thereafter, in the first copyright advertisement ever published by a store, Wanamaker announced his four cardinal points: *full guarantee, one price, cash payment, cash returned.* The advertisement contained a very detailed explanation as to how the plan would be carried out and firmly assured the public that no secrets would be kept from them, that only honest, truthful and fair dealings would mark any business owned and controlled by Wanamaker. It was what one observer called "the platform of modern business" begun by Wanamaker in the 1870s.

The following chapter describes the third phase of Wanamaker's growing empire as it moved beyond the confines of the "Downtown" business area of Philadelphia and expanded its merchandise inventory. It became a store that offered "Everything from Everywhere for Everybody."

The Genesis of
Department Stores

JOHN WANAMAKER HAS OFTEN BEEN CALLED the originator of the department store. He never accepted the honor. The idea seemed to develop simultaneously in both Europe and the United States when merchants endeavored to increase the number of customers in their stores: more products for sale would certainly attract more customers. It was Wanamaker, however, who capitalized on this idea and best demonstrated how it could be done.

In 1861, when he and his brother-in-law, Nathan Brown, started Oak Hall, a men's and boys' clothing store at Sixth and High Streets in Philadelphia, most retail shops limited themselves to one line of goods. The bootmaker, the milliner, the jeweler and the druggist all had their shops lining the streets and alley-ways, and the typical shopper spent a great deal of time going from store to store to purchase goods. When the population was small, a day's shopping spree could be an enjoyable time seeing old friends and keeping up with the latest happenings of the community. But as the population grew rapidly in Philadelphia, from 81,000 in 1800 to 408,000 in 1850, the streets got more crowded and shopping became a time-consuming task.

With an eye always to the future, young Wanamaker expanded his business and opened a second store on Chestnut Street above Eighth in 1869 following the death of his partner. His business increased steadily as the public responded to his advertisements and to the quality and price of his merchandise. He was gaining a reputation for reliability of goods, truthfulness in advertising, and customer satisfaction. What more could a businessman ask?

A deeply religious man, he believed his faith demanded that he devote himself one-hundred percent to any given task or responsibility.

He said, "Hardly any businessman is half what he might be." And, "No day seems long enough to those who love their work." He loved his work and was not satisfied with being less than what he could be. Neither he nor the world could anticipate what that would mean in the years ahead, but time would tell. While he was still in his mid-thirties, this man of vision saw the potential for businesses that one day would surround Philadelphia's new city hall.

When William Penn, founder of Philadelphia, laid out the street plan for his new city in 1682, streets ran east and west or north and south, creating a city of square blocks. Four of them he designated as parks on which nothing could be built; the land was to be preserved for the enjoyment of the citizens. Ultimately, they were named Rittenhouse Square, Logan Square, Washington Square and Franklin Square. Centre Square was in the middle of the four, where Broad and Market Streets intersect.

From 1800 to 1825 the City Water Works, which pumped water from the Schuylkill River to the reservoir located on the present site of the Philadelphia Museum of Art on the Parkway, was located on Centre Square. But times were changing. Development of the inner city meant that a new City Hall would be built on Centre Square and trains would no longer be able to carry their cargo on tracks running on Market Street from the Delaware to the Schuylkill rivers. In anticipation of this, the

Site of the John Wanamaker store, Thirteenth and Market Streets, Philadelphia, as it appeared in 1875

Pennsylvania Railroad freight sheds at Thirteenth and Market Streets were vacated by 1874.

In the same year, the Franklin Institute of Science used the empty freight sheds to celebrate its Centennial for a science fair. But the obsolete depot seemed to appeal to no one on a long-term basis.

Yet John Wanamaker had a dream; he bought the Depot in November 1875 for $505,000. Although there did not seem to be any urgent need for the building or grounds, that did not deter him from planning for the future. As he said, "Success is never an haphazard affair." If his business continued its growth, which was his intention and determination, he would soon need more space, and the old depot offered him plenty. Moreover, nothing could be better than to relocate his growing business at the future crossroads of Philadelphia, which he called "the city of opportunity."

THE MOODY-SANKEY MEETINGS

THOUGH THE LOCATION SEEMED CONSIDERABLY TOO FAR WEST of the retail business-hub of the city at that time, an unexpected event occurred that soon brought the depot to the attention of thousands upon thousands.

While Wanamaker was on a business and vacation trip to Europe in 1875, a group of religious businessmen, all friends of his, sought to bring evangelists Dwight L. Moody and Ira D. Sankey to Philadelphia for revival meetings. The largest covered facility in the city was the old freight depot at Thirteenth and Market Streets. And Wanamaker let them use it without cost. He said, "The new store can wait for a few months for its opening, the Lord's business comes first."

Rushing home from Europe, Wanamaker joined the committee and helped to purchase 8,904 seats for the congregation and 1,304 for the choir. (He always disliked round numbers.) He provided accommodations for Moody in his own home and paid all Moody's personal expenses. He attended every service during the two-month winter campaign, except for the times he was at Bethany, the Sunday School and church he had started. It is estimated that more than a million people attended the meetings, and Wanamaker sat on the platform each evening.

People began to realize how easy it was to get to Thirteenth and Market Streets. Equally important, they came to know the name of John Wanamaker. He was now ready to open his third store. When the Moody revival ended on January 21, 1876, Wanamaker's carpenters moved in within hours and began to remodel the old railroad freight station or as he named it, "The Grand Depot," the largest men's and boys' clothing store in the world.

Not only did he have the advantage of the impact of the revival meetings in publicizing his new location, he had the added benefit of the upcoming U.S. Centennial Exposition of 1876, which he served as Director of the Board of Finance. Knowing that large crowds would be coming to Philadelphia, his store advertisements were directed to out-of-town tourists. He printed over a million copies of a booklet describing the store and had them distributed to the Centennial visitors. The exterior architecture of his Grand Depot looked remarkably similar to the main buildings of the Exposition, with banners flying from the tops of flag poles high on the roof.

Wanamaker was occasionally accused of using his prominent position on the Moody and Centennial Committees for self-gain. But the charge seems unfair; he simply had the good sense to relate one event to another without abusing either.

THE UNITED STATES CENTENNIAL CELEBRATION

THE INTERNATIONAL EXHIBITION OF 1876, as it was formally called, began at 10:15 a.m. on Wednesday, May 10th with the arrival of General Ulysses S. Grant, President of the United States. Though the day had started with clouds and rain, the sun was shining brightly by mid-morning for the opening festivities. Crowds of people jammed tightly together with every eye directed toward the many distinguished guests seated on the large platform built for 4000 persons in front of the Art Gallery, known today as Memorial Hall. Seated next to the President was Dom Pedro II, the Emperor of Brazil, accompanied by the Empress. As each foreign representative was conducted to the platform, the grand orchestra played the appropriate national airs—eighteen altogether.

Following the orchestral performance of "The Centennial Grand March," composed by Richard Wagner, and a lengthy invocation by Methodist Bishop Matthew Simpson, a grand chorus sang the "Centennial Hymn" written for the occasion by John Greenleaf Whittier. But when the speeches began, few were able to hear due to the lack of amplification. After the address of President Grant, the outdoor cere-

Interior of the old Pennsylvania Railroad freight depot used for the Moody and Sankey revival meetings, November 21, 1875 to January 21, 1876

monies came to a close with a 100-gun artillery salute from George's Hill at the western edge of the grounds. The President then led the dignitaries to the nearby Main Exposition Building and to other exhibits in Machinery Hall.

John Wanamaker, as a director, had been seated on the platform for one of the most memorable events of his life. He was only thirty-eight and could hardly have been free from the thoughts of how wonderful it would be if all these people stopped by his Grand Depot before they left town.

THE GRAND DEPOT

JUST FOUR DAYS EARLIER, ON MAY 6, the doors of his new two-acre store had been thrown open, and many already referred to it as "the Centennial Annex." His employees, all well-trained and looking their best, were ready with stocks worth more than a half-million dollars. When the people came, they were as fascinated with the size of the big store as they were with anything they had seen at the Fair Grounds. They spent their money and told others about it. One of the salesmen jotted down some of the customers' remarks which Wanamaker then printed in his advertisements as follows:

> "Why, this reminds me of a Western prairie! It's most as big."

> "This is bigger than the Centennial itself. Why, an institution
> of this size would clothe the whole of Missouri." [1]

As the Centennial celebration neared the closing date of November 10, Wanamaker knew that something must be done to keep business from dropping off when people stopped coming to town. His remedy was "The New Kind of Store." Though he had sold only men's and boys' clothing up to this point, he now decided to add some items for women. First, there were shoes, then rubber raincoats, hosiery, gloves and trunks, just to mention a few.

On March 12, 1877 a momentous event occurred as Wanamaker expanded to the selling of dry goods. The entire floor space of the Grand Depot was re-designed in the shape of an enormous wheel with a 90-foot circular counter at the center. Aisles, 196 feet in length, radiated to the four corners of the store. One-hundred twenty-nine counters were arranged in concentric circles with 1400 stools placed in front for the convenience of the customers. Sitting-rooms and parlors provided comfort not found in other establishments.

Emphasizing the advantages of goods sold under one roof, the publicity announcements noted a variety of departments including—

A. Black and colored silks;
B. Mourning goods;
C. Flannels and domestics;
D. Linens and House Furnishing goods;
E. Upholstery;
F. Ladies suits, coats and shawls;
G. Custom Department, to make to order.

For the women who did not wish to make their own clothes or who could not afford the expense of a dress-maker, ready-made clothing could also be purchased.

The "New Kind of Store" had become a reality. On the Saturday before it opened (he didn't advertise on Sunday), Wanamaker, in his newspaper ad asked,

Will the people come on Monday, or at their leisure, and see what we have done?

They came! Thousands upon thousands. His doormen made an actual count of 71,106. It was a crowd so large that his 654 employees in the store had more customers than they could handle. At one point, Wanamaker and his chiefs even considered closing the doors. And all this took place on the single floor of the Grand Depot.

The great response was evidence of the trust people had in the man and his new system of business with the four basic principles he advertised:

First: Return of money if buyer returns goods in
         ten days uninjured,
Second: The guarantee to each buyer stating terms of sale,
Third: No second price,
Fourth: Any article, (including cut goods) may be
         exchanged if desired, within two weeks of purchase.

WANAMAKER'S POLICIES, accepted as normal a hundred years later, were revolutionary in 1877. Many storekeepers were disturbed and angry by these policies which they thought to be unreasonable and impractical. Neither did they want the pressure to fall in line with his policies. Some were openly hostile. Some ridiculed Wanamaker in mock advertisements:

> Billions of Millions, more or less, have visited our immense emporium during the first week of its existence and the mammoth headquarters of monopoly is now an established fact and must remain a monument to the gullibility of the public as long as there is a public to be gulled.[2]

Wanamaker, however, was not to be discouraged nor distracted by such jealousy. Even a three-column editorial in the *Sunday Mercury*[3] ridiculing the Wanamaker system and giving the store just three months grace before the sheriff stepped in could not destroy the determination of Wanamaker to hold to his ideals. With the encouragement of a few personal friends, he weathered a very difficult summer and fall when he was short of money and some suppliers would not sell him merchandise.

He believed that the public must be served in the most efficient manner possible. Advertising in *The Public Ledger*, he wrote:

> In one sense it is the people's store, owned and managed by John Wanamaker, who only benefits himself and his partners through the benefits secured by the store for the people.[4]

At another time he reiterated his goals by stating:

> The Founder always believed two things; First, that the prosperity of this business would assist the general prosperity of business in the city; Second, that the millions of people who were not stockkeepers had some rights to be considered in the advantages of better stocks to select from, lower prices brought about by certain economies and a much more generous service than was customarily in old time. These two fundamental beliefs have been proven to be correct.[5]

John Wanamaker store, Philadelphia, 1902

Business grew steadily, though not without its valleys and peaks, criticisms and commendations. In 1884 it was reported that 50,000 people entered the store daily and were served by more than 3,000 employees. The Mail Order Department received a thousand letters every day. It was the largest retail store in America; even Marshall Fields in Chicago did not compare with the John Wanamaker store in Philadelphia.

It had been necessary to enlarge the store by the acquisition of several adjoining properties. Once he succeeded in owning the entire block bounded by Market, Chestnut, Thirteenth and Juniper Streets, Wanamaker was able to get city permission to close Kelly Street, which had actually divided the store in half. He then filled the entire space with merchandise.

Other major developments included the addition of a basement and galleries, increasing total floor-space to eight acres, and a fresh air ventilating system (cool air that had been passed through sprays of water) that lowered the in-store temperature by ten or twelve degrees during hot summer months.

By the summer of 1885 the critical years at the Grand Depot had passed, and it soon became the first department store in the United States to exceed $10 million dollars in sales in one year. Wanamaker was now ready to relinquish his two stores at Sixth and Market and 818-822 Chestnut Streets to his brothers William H., Samuel M., and F. Marion, who had been managing them quite favorably. He could now devote himself full-time to the Thirteenth and Market Street store, his crown jewel, with the assistance of his favored employee Robert C. Ogden and his older son Thomas who had recently graduated from Princeton and was anxious to show his father his ability.

THE POSTMASTER GENERAL

FOUR YEARS LATER, in a surprising move, Wanamaker, though devoted to his business, accepted the call of President Harrison to become Postmaster General of the United States. Throughout the preceding year he had labored enthusiastically for the Republican Party, which had sought him for his financial support, widespread influence and popularity. Confident that Thomas and Ogden were sufficiently competent to manage the store in his absence, he moved to Washington and immersed himself in an attempt to reform the Postal System, a story told elsewhere in this book.

When he returned to Philadelphia in 1893, there seemed to be less need for his oversight of the store, and he had more of a desire to undertake something else. Unlike his political experience in the Post Office Department, the new project would have to be one in which he had total control and could act as he deemed wise.

THE CHALLENGE OF NEW YORK

UPON HEARING THAT THE FORMER A. T. STEWART retail dry-goods and clothing store in New York City was available for purchase in 1896, he quickly left his political speechmaking for the McKinley campaign in western Pennsylvania and took a night train to New York, dreaming all the way of the possibilities that lay ahead. A long-time admirer of Stewart, who had been one of the first merchants to help him get started in 1861 in Oak Hall, Wanamaker felt indebted for Stewart's help. In addition, he had never forgotten the day when Stewart, sympathetic to his mission,

Rotunda, John Wanamaker store, New York, 1910

handed him a $1000 check for the Bethany Sunday School in its early days.

During Stewart's lifetime, there had been a strong similarity between his business and Wanamaker's in Philadelphia. The business, now defunct, had enjoyed a reputation unequaled in the city as a "store that cared." One can appreciate the optimism of Wanamaker who believed that he could breathe new life into the old establishment despite the competition of the R. H. Macy store and others. Sentiment was mixed with challenge.

Wanamaker purchased the store, despite its location at Ninth and Broadway at a time when the business trend was to move uptown, and re-opened it just a month before Christmas. He took Ogden with him and left his son Thomas in charge of the Philadelphia store. In New York he entered a strange, difficult and different business world than he had experienced in the city on the Delaware. Nevertheless, he was confident that just as he had overcome numerous obstacles and the ridicule of others in the past, he would also succeed in his new venture. It was a challenge he could not and would not refuse.

He was not oblivious, however, to the differences in the two cities and the need to adapt the Wanamaker principles of merchandising without sacrificing values or integrity. But in just three years the business succeeded sufficiently so that he was able to take an extended vacation to Europe, which he would not have done had the business been in danger. In fact, growth was so rapid that more space was soon needed, and almost from the beginning he dreamed and planned for expansion.

When speaking at the commencement program at the Perkiomen Seminary in June 1902 he said:

> I have for five years been trying to find some way to put more stories on the building in New York City, but I can not do it.

Apparently the foundations of the old five-story building were not strong enough; at least not strong enough to bear the size of the building he wished to construct. So, as in Philadelphia, he purchased all the properties in the adjoining block and in 1906 began to build another sixteen-story addition across the street. With considerable fanfare he connected the upper floors of the two buildings with an overhead double-decked walkway that he dubbed "The Bridge of Progress." In addition, there were underground passageways for customers, employees and the moving of merchandise.

As could be expected, the new building included an auditorium three stories high that could seat 1500 people on the main floor and gallery. A large four-manual pipe organ became the center of attraction for numerous free public concerts.

The mercantile world was overwhelmed when Wanamaker announced the opening of "The House Palatial," a fully furnished, twenty-two room private home, with halls, staircases, and a summer garden, all built within the store as a model for "a family of taste and wealth." More than a million people visited it during the first year. Forty-four other furnished rooms throughout the store also displayed home decorations and furnishings representing various periods, styles and prices appealing to the broad interests of homeowners.

Stewart's onetime "Palace of Business" paled in comparison to the new Wanamakers. Following a visit to the new emporium, Elbert Hubbard described it in his unique manner:

> It is a Moving Pagent of Merchandise and Art, presenting a Business Exposition that outstages in many ways not only the great Centennial of 1876, but even the later greater expositions of the world. The older building is a "Woman's Store" devoted to women's fashions and luxuries with the "Au Quatrieme," a museum-like exposition of antiques, glass and objects of art.
>
> The first floor of the new building is a "Man's Store."
>
> The lower floors of both buildings are the "Downstairs Store," where economy joins hands with quality and satisfaction, forming a trinity hard to beat.
>
> The remaining fifteen stories of the new building are called "Galleries," where are displayed the wonders of mine and forest, loom and workshop from every corner of the globe, and with all that talent, skill and human ingenuity can add or invent, in bronze, marble, canvass, fabric or textile.[6]

It seems utterly astounding that simultaneously in Philadelphia, Wanamaker was building a new twelve-story store on the original site of the Grand Depot, constructing it in three sections, one at a time, so as not to disrupt the normal flow of business. Seven years passed before it was finally completed in 1911.

As Wanamaker approached seventy years of age, it appears that he anticipated leaving his sons two great stores, with Thomas in Philadelphia and Rodman in New York. But circumstances do not always conform to expectations. Several events occurred that made the next years the most difficult time of his life.

THE DEATH OF HIS ELDEST SON THOMAS—1861-1908

THOMAS BECAME SERIOUSLY ILL with devastating effects that hindered his ability to manage the business in Philadelphia. While realizing his own limitations, he felt that his father was unwilling to face up to the certain future. His letter of December 17, 1906 is so revealing and sad:

> My Dear Father:
>
> As an opportunity seems to be lacking for you and me to talk alone what I have in my mind, I will write it. As I informed you on the 4th of November last, that at the positive command of my medical advisors I determined to sever my relations with this business at the end of next month and indicated to you in part my reluctance in so doing and taking a step which means so much to me in every way and one I would not think of unless it were a matter I consider of life for a limited time, or certain death in a short time.
>
> As time is passing by very quickly these busy days, I wish you would have somebody get in shape the legal steps necessary which will give you the slightest trouble to put this into effect. Of course, it is useless to assure you or anybody here of my continued concern in this place, and I am your son,
>
> Thomas [7]

How the elder Wanamaker reacted or what he wrote in reply is unknown, but three days later Thomas wrote again:

> Dear Father,
>
> I have your letter and am sorry not to have seen you. I can only reiterate what I have already twice informed you of, namely, my decision to retire from all active business on Feb.1 next. I trust you will make it as easy as I have always

intended it should be. With the assistance of the organization about you, with the building of which I have had so much to do, it will give you not a particle of trouble or anxiety. But you will have to make plans which perhaps may not be left to the last moment to put into execution. And I am your son,

Thomas [8]

Leaving the business a short time later, Thomas began an extended trip with his mother, but while in Egypt he became seriously ill, was taken to Europe for medical assistance, and died in Paris. The distress of his father seemed almost unbearable, but John was determined to plod on ahead. Thomas had brilliantly managed the financial matters of the store for almost twenty years and had provided a positive restraint to the limitless idealism of his father. Now the burden of responsibility for John Wanamaker grew much heavier.

Also at this time, Robert C. Ogden, whom John called his "resident partner" in New York and who had been in ill health, found it necessary to retire at the age of seventy-one. Relying totally upon his other son Rodman who had returned from managing the overseas European purchasing office in Paris, John noted:

We two are the whole team—and we do a lot of pulling, for a two-horse team. [9]

Realizing that all of these things happened at once, the death of his son Thomas, the retirement of his partner Ogden, the added burden of simultaneously building two new large stores in Philadelphia and New York, as well as the loss of his country mansion by fire, one might well ask, "What else could possibly happen to affect the spirit of this man?" Students of history know the answer: The financial panic of 1907! It was devastating to numerous businesses and threatened to destroy Wanamaker as well.

Despite what had seemed to be "good times" across the nation at the beginning of 1907, the effect of the San Francisco earthquake of 1906 upon the investments of insurance companies coupled with several other economic factors, caused businesses everywhere to plummet. People stopped buying anything except bare necessities. Wanamaker faced the same problems as all others, and he had been counting on an increase in sales to cover the costs of his new buildings.

Even as rumors of his impending failure flowed freely, he received assurances of assistance from friends who had seen him overcome other major obstacles in the past. They were confident he would be the victor again. In his newspaper advertisements he heralded messages of hope and advised the public to stop withdrawing their money from the banks and hoarding it.

His deep religious faith during the time of crisis remained the same as in times of great success. In his diary he wrote:

> I am just going on day after day with a heart strong in
> the belief that the Heavenly Father has me in his keeping and
> will guide me to do for me what is best.[10]

Finally in 1909, after a long siege, business began an upturn and Wanamaker celebrated his personal victory in overcoming the financial crises affecting both stores. Combining skill and religious faith he had weathered the storm.

For months he had devoted himself to the New York business, living temporarily at the Plaza, commuting frequently to the Philadelphia store, and spending weekends at Lindenhurst and Bethany. Now he longed to be back home. It was his first love.

RODMAN WANAMAKER IN NEW YORK

HIS SON RODMAN, ACCUSTOMED TO THE LIFE OF PARIS, seemed the most suitable candidate to take over the management of the New York store. (This had been the original plan of his father.) Taking up residence there, Rodman soon won the respect and admiration of the business and civic communities in New York as his father had done in Philadelphia. As business flourished and demands upon his time increased, he nevertheless accepted the mayor's appointment as Deputy Police Commissioner with responsibility as New York's official greeter of distinguished guests including kings, queens, cardinals and later, in 1918, the military forces returning home from the battlefields of Europe.

Whatever Rodman did, whether building the Eternal Light War Memorial in Madison Square, sponsoring the North American Indian Expeditions to the West, offering to construct a gigantic memorial to the American Indian on the Hudson shore, building a giant hydroplane to cross the Atlantic or sponsoring Admiral Byrd's flights, all favorably impacted the great business enterprise which carried his father's name but whose success was the result of their combined efforts. In some respects, the thirty-two acre New York emporium, under his guiding hand, moved into the lead ahead of the Philadelphia store.

Leaving Rodman in New York, John Wanamaker returned to Philadelphia to prepare for the completion of the new building and the Golden Jubilee celebration of 1911. Few individuals have the luxury of looking back over an endeavor they pioneered fifty years earlier as he did. Moreover, this remarkable milestone was not the finish line as in a race nor the capstone as of a building; rather it was the opening of another era in the life of a store whose first day's business grossed only $24.67 but now had become a multi-million dollar enterprise. As chronicled in the 1911 *Golden Book* of the Wanamaker Stores:

> It is the history of a business that has distributed into the homes of the civilized world more than half a billion dollars worth of merchandise. Nearly a hundred million more than half a billion. A business that has given remunerative employ-ment to over 150,000 individual workers. Whose census today reaches a maximum of over 15,000. Whose stocks total over fourteen millions of dollars. [11]

*Setting the capstone, new Wanamaker building, Philadelphia, June 11, 1910
(John Wanamaker standing on box)*

THE JUBILEE MARCH—1911

BEGINNING ON THE FIRST DAY OF MARCH, one celebration followed another to mark the half-century milestone. The store was filled with exhibits of clothing and costumes, toys, harpsichords and pianos, furnishings, perfumes and soaps, depicting fifty years of progress and change in styles and manufacturing.

Anniversary Day, March 13, began with a breakfast Wanamaker had planned for his business chiefs before the store opened. The tables were turned when he found himself being honored by his executives. As a token of their friendship and admiration, they presented him with a single red rose and a sealed envelope which was not to be opened until Jubilee Day, October 28.

Surprised and moved by their affection, Wanamaker called it not simply an anniversary breakfast but a wedding breakfast, saying, "I thank God for the privilege of having lived with you."

THE CRYSTAL TEA ROOM

APRIL BROUGHT ANOTHER EVENTFUL DAY when the Crystal Tea Room was first opened to the public. As Philadelphia's largest restaurant, and one of the largest in the world with 22,000 square feet, it seated 1500 persons at one time. Located on the ninth floor and overlooking neighboring buildings, it offered an unbroken eastern view of the city, the Delaware River and New Jersey. The beauty and light of its many crystal chandeliers, the twenty-foot-high columned ceilings, its oak woodwork and oak parquet floors were unmatched anywhere. Several adjoining dining rooms, the Coronation Tea Room, Imperial Blue Room and the Golden Jubilee Room, provided more intimate dining for private groups. Twenty-four elevators gave direct access to the Tea Room from all floors of the store. It was a far cry from the original restaurant, the Dairy, which had opened in 1876 at the Grand Depot with just four tables and sixteen chairs.

JUBILEE NIGHT

JUBILEE NIGHT WAS CELEBRATED on October 28, at the close of business, as 6800 employees of the Philadelphia store assembled in their own sections for the procession to the Grand Court, headed by the Seventh Regiment Military Band of the New York store. Passing in review before John Wanamaker and his personal guests, his employees then joined with a 1000-voice chorus, the Regimental Band, The John Wanamaker Commercial Institute Military Bands, the thundering Great Organ and an audience of 30,000, singing,

> America! America!
> God shed his grace on thee. [12]

Wanamaker, the poor boy from South Philadelphia, had achieved his success in America, the land of opportunity, for which he was ever grateful. One can only imagine the thrill that enveloped him at that moment.

The highlight of the evening occurred when he opened the sealed envelope he had received from his business chiefs in March. Inside he found the deed of his birthplace which had been purchased by the 13,000 employees of both stores as a token of their affection for him. Following his acceptance speech in the Grand Court, which was unable to accommodate all the employees, he went to four other locations in the building where he personally spoke to the rest of his Store Family.

As a memento of the occasion, Wanamaker later printed a 138-page booklet, "I Was There, Philadelphia, October 28, 1911," containing many tributes and Wanamaker's acceptance speech which was distributed to all. It was not unusual of him to be thoughtful of others as he stated:

> I am glad always to be linked to you. I believe in you. I have reason to believe in you, when so many of you occupying high positions in the house, were boys and girls here, away back in the years.

Giving tribute to his secretary who had been in his employ for forty years, he offered a 225-acre farm in the nearby suburbs as the site for a retirement home for needy, aged and retired employees, calling it the *Howard S. Jones Residence House.*

Additionally, he announced that he would build another institution upon the land of his birthplace and name it the *Robert C. Ogden Children's Hospital,* as a tribute to his former partner and associate.

IN THE FOLLOWING MONTH, The Merchants of America gave public recognition to Wanamaker at a luncheon in New York at Sherry's. More than 125 distinguished merchants, politicians, educators, and publishers from across America gathered in his honor and presented him with a two-foot-high silver loving cup.

Following many speeches that highlighted his remarkable contribution to the mercantile world, Wanamaker spoke of the pride he had in the accomplishments of "The Honorable Merchants of the United States." Never at a loss for an appropriate word, he commented,

> These are they who initiated and maintain, by manufacture and distribution, the business which makes the life and Prosperity of the Nation. But for the commerce of the land, the bankers could not use their money, nor could the railroads be supported by freights and travelers. We are at the very heart of the prosperity of our country. [13]

PRESIDENT TAFT DEDICATES THE NEW BUILDING

THE JUBILEE YEAR CELEBRATION did not end until December 30 when President William Howard Taft arrived from Washington in his private railroad car "The Mayflower" to dedicate the newly completed twelve-story granite building at Thirteenth and Market Streets. Earlier in the year Wanamaker had been the President's weekend guest at the White House and slept in the Lincoln Room. While there, he reflected upon his years as Postmaster General and commented, "We met here for the Cabinet in Harrison's time."

At the dedication he contended that the President's visit to Philadelphia was not of his doing and that he had not spoken a single word about it to him, but that the President came of his own volition.

Wanamaker escorted Taft from the Broad Street Station past throngs of people who had gathered to catch just a glimpse of the President. Then he and Taft entered the Grand Court where more than 30,000 guests greeted them. In the presence of Rudolph Blankenburg, Mayor of Philadelphia; Pennsylvania Governor John K. Tener; U.S. Senator Boies Penrose; members of Congress and the judicatories; Daniel H. Burnham,

John Wanamaker store, Philadelphia, 1911

Esq., architect; and numerous other distinguished persons, Taft gave his dedicatory address. Referring to the unique development of the store through fifty years he said:

> It seems to have acquired its own personality, different even from that of the Founder, so that he finds himself bound by the very rules he created and the traditions that have worked to eminent success. [14]

At seventy-three, Wanamaker was in his glory. Never before had the Chief Executive of the United States singled out a privately owned enterprise and recognized it with such honor. As he stood on the raised platform with the President at his side, directly before him was the massive bronze eagle that symbolized his own spirit, "to soar to the highest sky and dare the fiercest storm." He had lived this motto for fifty years—a remarkable record.

It is not surprising that, with the two new buildings in Philadelphia and New York now completed, the strong leadership of his son Rodman, a management staff well-trained over many years, and political ambitions diminished, Wanamaker decided to spend more time vacationing, enjoying the winter months on a private houseboat provided by his son—a luxury he would not have allowed himself. But even on the waters of the Gulf of Mexico he maintained contact with the store through daily correspondence, receiving the latest sales and financial reports and sending his hand-written editorials for the newspaper advertisements, a practice he maintained until his death.

Taft plaque in Grand Court

An Advertising Genius

ADVERTISING WAS THE LIFE-BLOOD of John Wanamaker's stores from the very beginning. Wanamaker did not believe in the old adage about building a better mousetrap and having people beat a path to one's door. Filled with optimism and a generous portion of self-confidence, he believed that crowds of people would come to his store and buy his merchandise only if he took the initiative and went to them by way of honest and eye-catching advertisements. Innovative, he devised advertising methods that were then adopted and followed by other merchants.

Wanamaker's advertising wizardry led his business from a small beginning to a phenomenal success and enormous personal fortune. He explained it in these words:

> Advertising is one of the chief elements of success, but not
> the chief. The chief element is getting what the people want.
> The advertisement is to tell them that I have it. [1]

At the end of the first day of business in 1861, Wanamaker and his partner, Nathan Brown, counted sales totaling $24.67. They put 67 cents into the cash box to make change the next day and spent $24.00 for advertising.

At first, Philadelphians saw huge 100-foot-long signs announcing that Wanamaker and Brown had opened their new store just up the street from Colonel Bennett's Tower Hall (the clothing establishment where young Wanamaker had worked four years earlier). The two partners called their venture "Oak Hall" to symbolize their store's anticipated growth (as a great oak tree develops from a tiny acorn) and to capitalize on its similarity to Tower Hall's name. Several stores in other cities also had the name Oak Hall, first introduced by George W. Simmons, a merchant in Boston in 1842.

With a flair for publicity, Wanamaker released large twenty-foot balloons with an announcement that anyone finding a balloon would be given a suit of clothes. One such balloon, landing in New Jersey, was caught among swamp bushes and reportedly frightened farmers who thought they had seen a strange animal or an elephant hiding in the brush. Of course, this heightened the public's interest in the store and its unusual form of advertising.

Colorful Oak Hall promotion cards straightforwardly announced: "Spring Clothing—the Largest Variety, the Lowest Prices," or "It will pay you to buy your Boy's Clothing at Oak Hall."

At times, a tally-ho carriage, drawn by six large, spirited horses, crisscrossed the city and countryside. The Oak Hall employees aboard, dressed in stylish fashion, blew their horns and distributed handbills. Wanamaker may have been one of the first to use "sandwich men," who walked about the city wearing advertising placards for his store.

The thrust of his unique advertising style was constantly to build bridges to span the chasm separating customers from merchants. Wanamaker used newspapers as a primary medium because in print he could emphasize the basic policies of his business. Honesty and fairness were foremost.

He announced first of all that his prices were fair, that his goods were reliable, and that "the store takes the side of the customer." Moreover, if customers were not satisfied for any reason, they could return the goods and receive their money back.

Spanning the chasm was a matter of being human, frank and straight to the point. In a memo to his advertising chief he advised:

> Your sole business as a writer for our advertising is to find out
> the truth regarding the merchandise and tell it in plain words
> and as briefly as you can. [2]

To sell an item was important, but to promote the characteristics of his store was of utmost significance. This emphasis continued when he opened his second store on Chestnut Street. An 1880 advertising trade-card asked the question, "How do we keep our customers?" "Treat them better than they expect and charge them less" was the answer. Promoting good-will and confidence and establishing a store personality was of far greater value, for Wanamaker, than simply telling what merchandise could be purchased at what price.

Wanamaker's third store opened just in time for the beginning of the U.S.Centennial Exposition in Fairmount Park in 1876. Wanamaker printed over a million handouts advertising the opening of the Grand Depot at Thirteenth and Market Streets, and thousands made their way there throughout the summer months.

Three years later he became the first merchant to place a full-page advertisement in the newspaper. [3] It was an endeavor to reach the largest number of people in the most economical manner. Its success caused him to say:

> If ever I have a Columbus monument for discovering any-thing, it will be for finding out that the only advertising of direct and instant benefit to both the merchant and the buyer is the daily newspapers of known circulation. [4]

Wanamaker signed a contract with the *Philadelphia Record* in the early 1890s for more than $100,000 for his daily ads. Nevertheless he admitted,

> I know that half the money I spend on advertising is wasted, but I don't know which half. [5]

In his ads, repetition was often used to catch the eye of the reader. From the top to the bottom of the page a single phrase like "Dry Goods" or "Oak Hall" was repeated as many as sixty, seventy or eighty times. It would have been almost impossible to overlook the ad as one flipped the pages even hurriedly. *McElroy's Philadelphia City Directory for 1865* carried a two-line Wanamaker Store advertisement at the top of every page, a variation of the repetition idea.

Another interesting innovation was the inclusion of the day's "weather report" in the ads long before that practice became a regular feature of newspapers. A typical prediction in 1890 cautiously announced, "The weather today is likely to be fair." [6]

An interesting advertisement for Old Folks Day stated:

> The man who forgets early friends and life-time relations pays a high price for prosperity. An anniversary of this store with-out them would have a hole in it. One of our Anniversary

Days is to receive and honor old friends who visit us. THIS IS THEIR DAY. Special programs throughout the Day, Guides, Rolling Chairs, French Revolution Puppet Show, Girls Chorus, Special Reception Rooms. [7]

Some ads included facts and figures to impress the public with the unmatched achievements of the Wanamaker store in its unending expansion. Shortly after the new building was constructed in 1911 a store booklet gave this description:

> The complete Wanamaker store in Philadelphia is 247 feet high, 480 feet long and 250 feet wide. It contains 30,000 tons of steel. It contains 24,000 tons of granite. It has 45 acres of floor space. It is the largest retail institution in the world. [8]

An anniversary day booklet reminisced and retold in picturesque detail the story of the opening of the Grand Depot in 1876.

> Everything for purchase is on one floor, on which

streams from every quarter of the sky-lighted roof, floods of light, so that, notwithstanding the vastness of the store, one sees at a glance almost just where the article is that is sought for. [9]

Among the wide variety of hand-out publicity materials were accordion-style folding fans, colorful picture postcards, double-folded tissue postcards (including one that when blown into expanded to form a model of the twelve-floor store building), souvenir spin cards for children with pictures of Santa Claus, facsimiles of a five-dollar bill with the announcement "You can buy a suit of clothes at Oak Hall from five dollars to sixty dollars...," and picture cards of Zulu warriors in loin cloths with spears and large shields emblazoned with "John Wanamaker & Co., finest clothing, lowest prices, invites competition...."

As business grew, numerous public relations programs in the store provided a new way of advertising. The construction of the auditorium in the Grand Depot, followed later in 1911 by Egyptian Hall and Greek Hall, created large meeting rooms for public events. The public was invited to attend free concerts and educational exhibitions such as "Napoleon," "The French Revolution" with tableaus and relics, "Monarchs and Beauties of the World," "Hiawatha," and "The North American Indians." Special celebrations included Grand Army Day, Pennsylvania Day, Scottish Day, Children's Day, and Great Authors of the World Day with personal appearances by Henry Van Dyke, Hugh Walpole, Joseph Lincoln, and others. Simultaneously, an exhibition of original and priceless manuscripts was displayed.

St. Patrick's Day, 1906 included a mid-day concert of the choir from the Church of the Gesu, an afternoon concert for children, the distribution of 156 genuine imported black thorns from Ireland as prizes along with 5760 genuine dundeens made of real Irish clay, 500 crochet-needles and spools of thread made in Ireland, thousands of oak cakes baked in Ireland for this special occasion, paper shamrocks, and an evening banquet tendered by the Friendly Sons of St. Patrick.

Presenting six beautiful imported shillalahs to the speakers at the banquet, Wanamaker said:

> As your members all believe in clubs, I thought that you might like to have as souvenirs these shillalahs, which I guarantee to be of genuine Irish growth, having been cut espe-

cially for me not far from Belfast. It is a good thing to have something ready when you take up the cudgels for the good causes that keep coming along. [10]

At most of the public events, various singing groups of employees or the chorus and band of the John Wanamaker Commercial Institute, composed of the young boys and girls of the store, provided music. The talent and camaraderie of the employees strongly promoted or "advertised" the store.

Reference has been made elsewhere in this book to the Wanamaker Art Gallery, the Eagle, the Crystal Tea Room and the Organ Concerts which also were significant advertising elements with tremendous drawing power.

At enormous personal cost, John Wanamaker offered a variety of cultural, educational and social opportunities that the public accepted with alacrity. As customers made their purchases to show their gratitude, both he and they profited.

The Wanamaker philosophy of advertising harmonized with Wanamaker's basic principle of serving customers in the best possible manner. Advertising was his way of keeping prices as low as possible. He summarized it by saying:

> The more goods a store sells, the more economically those goods can be made and distributed. Presuming the merchant takes only his just profit, the greater return for their money will the people get. [11]

Tell It  Like It Is!

FOLLOWING THE EXAMPLE OF THE FOUNDER who said, "First—we shall sell goods for what they really are, and Second—for what they are actually worth," the advertising chief at Wanamaker's was asked to write an ad for men's ties.

The tie salesman suggested that the ad read, "You can have these beautiful ties for 25 cents reduced from $1.00." The ad man asked, "How good are they?" The reply was, "They're not much good at all." Going back to his desk, the ad man wrote:

Men's ties.
They're not as good as they look
But they're good enough.
25 cents.

Sales became so great that the store had to buy additional cheap ties for almost a month to meet the demand. [1]

A PERPETUAL FOUNTAIN
of new syles in
Neckwear and Furnishing for
Men
is the **John Wanamaker Store.**

The Great Organ

MUSIC LOVERS FROM AROUND THE WORLD have marveled at the magnificence of the Great Organ at John Wanamakers in Philadelphia. It is the largest in the world and has been played daily for more than eighty years, beginning on June 22, 1911.

John Wanamaker loved music and gave it a prominent place in both his business and his church. To him, music possessed both spiritual and cultural value, not to mention its importance in drawing people into the store, which led to increased sales. He had first purchased a small organ for the Grand Depot when he was selling what he called "house melodeons in our piano department." The interest of the people grew so strong in the free musical programs offered each day that it was obvious the programs would have to continue in the new emporium. A much larger organ would be needed for the Grand Court, which he called "a great Cathedral."

Wanamaker relied heavily upon the suggestion of his son Rodman, who had learned to play the piano and organ at Bethany and had become a devotee and patron of the fine arts. They decided to build "the finest organ in the world" and offer its music to their customers.

They were told that it would take a long time to build an instrument large enough to meet their desires. Their sources also informed them of a large organ that had been on exhibit in Festival Hall at the Louisiana Purchase Exposition of 1904 in St. Louis. The Kansas City Municipal Auditorium had been its intended final home, but the contract had been voided by the city. Following the Exposition, the organ had been placed in storage where Wanamaker found it.

Wanamaker sent George Till, an organ technician in the store, to St. Louis to evaluate the organ's suitability for the Grand Court. Accepting Till's recommendation, Wanamaker lost no time in purchasing it and having it shipped to Philadelphia. Transported on thirteen freight cars it arrived at the reconstructed store on August 23, 1909.

The Great Organ

Grand Court, John Wanamaker store, Philadelphia

The Great Organ with builder W. B. Fleming, John Wanamaker store, Philadelphia
(Courtesy of Henry Baecker)

Wanamaker also engaged the services of W. B. Fleming, the original builder from the Los Angeles Art Organ Company, who came to Philadelphia to supervise its reconstruction. Fleming remained in that capacity until he retired in 1927. Almost immediately, the organ was enlarged with numerous additions to pipes and stops along with a new five-manual console. The present six-manual console was installed in 1928 and the organ was finished about 1931. Mary Vogt, selected by Rodman Wanamaker when she was only a teenager, was the store organist from 1917 until her retirement in 1966.

A descriptive booklet, distributed for many years in the store, stated:

Everything is within the organist's reach. It has 451 stops and 964 controls. There are forty-two accessories for the feet and 729 tilting tablets operated by remote control from 168 pistons under manual keys of which there are forty-six masters and forty-six reversibles. [1]

Various organ chambers are located not only on the second, third and fourth floors behind the enormous organ-screen on the Chestnut Street side of the Grand Court, but on the seventh floor at both the Market Street and Chestnut Street sides as well. The string division occupies the largest single organ chamber ever constructed, measuring 60' long, 30' wide and 20' high. Some pipes, too tall for the room, have been laid sideways on the floor with one placed upon another. The 30,067 pipes vary in size from the smallest, just three-quarters of an inch long, to the largest wood pipe, 32 feet long, 27 inches wide and 32 inches deep. The heaviest one weighs 1,735 pounds. The largest metal pipe is 37 feet, 9 inches long and 17 inches in diameter. A piano, harp, celesta, gongs, metalophone and two sets of chimes, major and minor, can also be played from the console.

In addition to several concerts by organists Charles Courboin, Pietro Yon and Marcel Dupre with the Philadelphia Orchestra under the baton of Leopold Stokowski, many other world-renowned organists have performed on this colossal instrument. Virgil Fox and Keith Chapman both produced recordings on the Wanamaker organ.

At this writing, a major rebuilding will soon provide the most up-to-date, state-of-the-art electronic control available. Unmatched in size and expressive sound, the magnificent Wanamaker organ, often called "the noblest musical instrument in the world," will continue to spread the joy of music to shoppers and visitors alike, just as John Wanamaker and his son had intended so many years ago.

The Munkacsy Paintings 10

TWO OF THE MOST FAMOUS PAINTINGS ever displayed at Wanamakers are "Christ Before Pilate" and "Christ on Calvary" by the celebrated Hungarian artist, Michael von Munkacsy. In 1882 he was called "the greatest painter of modern times."[1] His two masterpieces—biblical epics—were first exhibited in several European cities, receiving unusual praise from art critics and the general public.

John Wanamaker visited the baron's home in Luxembourg in 1887 and purchased "Christ Before Pilate" shortly thereafter. In the following year he acquired "Christ on Calvary." Both paintings were first exhibited in the United States at the Twenty-third Street Tabernacle in New York City. During the next five months they were sent to several cities throughout the nation where they were seen by hundreds of thousands of people.

For many years the paintings, which Wanamaker considered his "most treasured possessions," were placed in the Grand Court of the Philadelphia store as part of the magnificent Easter displays. They were also exhibited by Wanamakers at the New York World's Fair in 1939.

"Christ Before Pilate" is 20 feet, 8 inches long by 13 feet, 6 inches wide. "Christ on Calvary" is 23 feet, 4 inches long by 14 feet, 2 inches wide. Both paintings, along with many others owned by Wanamakers and displayed in the Wanamaker Art Gallery and throughout the store, were sold in 1988.

Presently, a part of the collection of Joey and Toby Tannenbaum, Toronto, Canada, "Christ Before Pilate" is on public display at the Joey and Toby Tannenbaum Opera Centre, Imperial Oil Theatre in Toronto.

"Christ on Calvary," owned by Julian and Pamela Beck of Washington, Connecticut, is currently exhibited at the Hungarian National Museum in Budapest, Hungary until the year 2000.

Christ Before Pilate, *Munkacsy, courtesy of Joey and Toby Tannenbaum*

Christ On Calvary, *Munkacsy, courtesy of Julian and Pamela Beck*

Meet Me at the Eagle

THE EAGLE IN THE GRAND COURT at the John Wanamaker store in Philadelphia has been a favorite meeting place for friends since 1911 when the new store was built. Its location is so well known that no one ever needs to say more than, "Meet me at the Eagle."

John Wanamaker bought the Eagle sometime after the close of the Louisiana Purchase Exposition of 1904 in St. Louis. There it stood in the Palace of Varied Industries dominating the entrance to the Court of Honor of the German Exhibition. [1]

Ordered by the Imperial German Commission, the Eagle, forged in bronze, is the work of the well-known and celebrated sculptor, August

Gaul of Berlin. It was manufactured in Frankfurt, Germany by Armbruester Brothers, notably called "Purveyors to His Majesty, the German Emperor." Instead of being cast-bronze, the eagle's head and body are formed of 5000 individually hand-crafted feathers which were hammered and bent while yet hot, giving an appearance of natural softness to each feather. The 2,500 pound eagle, stands on a large granite pedestal with its wings joined at rest.

Today, it majestically occupies the center of Wanamaker's Grand Court and remains as a familiar Philadelphia symbol of friendship, while people still say, "Meet me at the Eagle."

The John Wanamaker
Commercial Institute

THE PHENOMENAL GROWTH OF THE "NEW KIND OF STORE" created by John Wanamaker provided employment for more than 1250 people by 1877. Because the principles, policies and procedures were different from those found in other retail stores, it was vital that each new employee be trained to follow the Wanamaker plan. The educational programs for employees began in 1878.

In the early years, Wanamaker himself had carefully selected individuals who shared his business ideas as well as his ethical and moral ideals. He also spent considerable time bringing together the "store family" at meetings where he personally challenged them with his lively speeches or with written messages compiled in small booklets. "How can we better serve the people?" he repeatedly asked. He wanted answers. He also exhorted them: "Never be content with the best when something better may be had." It was a theme he often repeated.

Wanamaker was not satisfied to teach only the older employees; he felt that the younger children in his employ also deserved educational opportunities. Many of them had not been able to attend public schools and some had been forced to enter early employment because of poverty at home. Others, of course, were looking for meaningful careers.

To meet those needs, The John Wanamaker Commercial Institute was founded on March 12, 1896. Courses of instruction included not only commercial history, banking, financing and bookkeeping, but also the more basic subjects of arithmetic, spelling, grammar, English composition, history and ethics, to name but a few.

At first, the school taught only the younger boys of the store who attended classes early in the morning before they went to their assigned jobs. A girls' branch was added later, and a senior boys' branch was developed as a night school. A school principal supervised the venture, which was conducted in well-lighted classrooms equipped with typical school furniture. Textbooks and writing materials were all provided by the store without cost to the students.

The boys in the Senior Branch, the first group to be called cadets, gained membership in the Cadet Corps by completing a prescribed course of instruction and giving satisfactory service in both store and school work as well as in preliminary military drill. From September to May the cadets met on Tuesday and Friday nights each week from 6:00 to 9:00 P.M. The store provided a free supper for them before they reported to class. Military drill was conducted for forty-five minutes one evening each week and for forty minutes on two mornings each week from 7:50 to 8:30 A.M. The school assembly, held at the beginning of each Friday evening session, was described as "an opportunity for the practice of public speaking and singing."

Every June, the three branches of the Institute (Girls', Junior Boys' and Senior Boys') each conducted Class Day Exercises to close the school year. Held in Egyptian Hall or University Hall, the graduation programs were typical of those held in public schools today with music provided by the Cadet Band and the Boys' and Girls' Choruses. The procession of the graduates began with "the colors of our Nation, our City, our store and our School." The Graduates Association and the school principal presented various prizes and certificates.

At the end of the school year, the graduating seniors made an expense-free three-day trip to Washington, D.C., with their teachers and military officers. It was a special treat the students anticipated throughout the year.

CAMP WANAMAKER

WANAMAKER ALSO PROVIDED A TWO-WEEK SUMMER VACATION for the boys and girls at "The Barracks," located at Island Heights, New Jersey, on Barnegat Bay near the Atlantic Ocean. Wanamaker, impressed by the healthful qualities found with pinewoods and salt air, purchased thirteen acres here in 1899 to be used as a campground for his youthful employees. Many of them would not otherwise have had a vacation. To Wanamaker, it meant the joy of investing in the lives of young people by helping to raise the standards of moral, ethical, mental and physical behavior in an environment of fun and games.

Camp Wanamaker, Island Heights, New Jersey

John Philip Sousa leading the cadet band of the John Wanamaker store, Philadelphia

When the campers left for their two-week vacation, Wanamaker personally gave them a send-off speech at the store. Then the campers, in their colorful cadet uniforms, marched down Market Street and boarded the Pennsylvania Railroad Ferry which crossed the Delaware River to Camden, New Jersey. From there they traveled by train, "a special with vestibuled cars," to Island Heights where they were joined by a similar contingent of cadets from the New York Wanamaker store. When they arrived at Barnegat Bay, the campers' luggage was loaded onto large farm wagons, and they marched to the camp. There the cadets settled into the camp's two-hundred tents (two to a tent).

Mornings began when the bugler sounded reveille at 7:00 A.M. Sitting-up exercises, clean-up, breakfast, assembly and inspection of quarters followed. The remainder of the day was filled with boating, sailing, fishing, crabbing, swimming, hiking, races, calisthenics, rifle practice, baseball, field and track events and other games. Evenings were spent in military drills, parades and band concerts until the bugle sounded taps at 10:30 P.M. and the campers fell asleep.

Religious services were held on Sundays. Occasionally there were trips to nearby towns such as Lakewood and Toms River.

The campers had been assigned to military companies and regiments with officers in charge when they arrived at camp. During the following two weeks, the companies competed against each other in various events and activities and were evaluated for their performance. Before the end of camp the companies were given appropriate recognition at an awards ceremony. Many cadets received medals for their outstanding performance.

For many of the youth the camp experience was unforgettable and the excitement lingered long. As one camper wrote, "Our trip back to Camden was a jolly one, each of us trying to talk louder and faster than the rest as we related our good times."

Wanamaker was proud of his cadets. During one of his visits to the Summer Camp at Island Heights on August 14, 1913, he wrote of his favorable impressions to his son Rodman:

> I am sitting under a tree on these Grounds, where it is raining now and then—watching the athletics. There are 150 Philadelphia boys and 97 New York boys. The possibilities apparent of this movement of yours to benefit the boys and girls impels me to see what can be done to forward this good work. [1]

It was not unusual for him to give Rodman the credit, whether or not he had initiated the idea, but he also had the vision to foresee the benefits for a nation approaching war as well as for the young people and the two stores.

WARS

IN 1898 WHEN THE UNITED STATES AND SPAIN WERE AT WAR, the Cadets were a well-organized, well-trained, and well-equipped force ready to answer the call to military service. Correspondence shows that Wanamaker offered the Governor of Pennsylvania "1000 men ready to report for service in 48 hours." He personally volunteered to command them in battle or to take "a subordinate place or go in the ranks." [2]

Wanamaker sent notification to all employees indicating that he would keep open their jobs, would continue their salaries and send it to their homes, if they would enlist. In the event of death, he promised to provide a $1,000 payment to their families. Over 2,000 employees and others volunteered in response to the notices he placed in the newspapers. He accepted only those who resided in the city and began to drill 907 of them in the nearby Armory. They were armed and equipped at Wanamaker's expense, only to hear that they were not needed because the war came quickly to an end.

During World War I, over 1400 employees of the New York and Philadelphia Wanamaker stores served in the military forces. Many of them were immediately appointed as officers because of the training they had already received as Wanamaker cadets. Wanamaker's own grandson, John, went to France with the 78th Division, was appointed Captain—a title he proudly carried for the rest of his life—and served as Exchange Officer and Intelligence Officer while there. He wrote to his grandfather:

> I've been across the wide blue sea. I've been at the Kaiser's Door. There's just one place more I'd like to be, and that's back at the Wanamaker store. [3]

Much to the sorrow of the "store family," thirty-four employees were killed on the field of battle. In May, 1919 Wanamaker unveiled a plaque in the Grand Court at the Philadelphia store with a single gold star commemorating the sacrifice of his employees for their country.

The ability to serve with distinction in the nation's military was only one result of the education provided by the John Wanamaker Commercial Institute. Right from the Institute's beginning, an esprit-de-corps developed among the store's young employees that enhanced the service they offered to the general public.

THE CADET LIFE-STYLE

"THE HANDBOOK FOR GUIDANCE OF THE J.W.C.I. CADETS" stated that "each new cadet must study and understand these rules, and, before entering a grade in the J.W.C.I., must satisfactorily pass a test in them."
Some of the rules in the Handbook referred to:

A. Daily duty regarding class assignments.
B. Lateness and Absence—classes not to be missed except by permission.
C. Mid-day intermission of 45 minutes.
D. Shopping regulations—not during store hours.
E. Pay day— Friday. [4]

The personal appearance of each cadet was a major concern, and cleanliness was insisted upon. Girls were required to wear "a plain black or dark blue skirt with a plain white waist, black stockings and black shoes." No colors were to be worn in collars, ties, beads or trimmings. Boys wore dark suits, white collar, dark tie, black shoes and stockings. Neither canvass shoes nor sweaters were permitted to be worn during business hours and hair was to be kept well-trimmed.

It is not surprising that a specific life-style was also created by expectation if not by regulation. In matters of conduct, it was expected that all would be quiet, dignified and businesslike. Prohibitions included eating on the job, chewing gum, the use of slang or bad English, marking on walls, fixing hair or nails, powdering in public, wasting time, and entertaining friends during business hours. Of course, politeness and courtesy were "signs of respect for others" as well as "of self-respect."

Pride in one's work was fundamental to John Wanamaker. He demonstrated it himself and believed that his employees would succeed in whatever they did if they performed their tasks with personal pride, self-discipline, commitment and enthusiasm.

In the Wanamaker system, employees were valued. All persons made a contribution no matter how small or routine their assignments. Successful employees were promoted to better positions as they gained education and their skills improved. Relatively few left Wanamakers for other places because Wanamakers was the best place to work in the city. Beyond the prestige of working there and free educational classes, employees received free medical attention and care from the store's physician. They were encouraged to use the recreational activities at the athletic field on the roof of the store equipped with tennis courts and running track, to sing in the chorus of 650 men, women, boys and girls, and to join the Minstrel Troupe or the Dramatic Club.

AMERICAN UNIVERSITY OF TRADE AND
APPLIED COMMERCE

OUT OF THE SMALL BEGINNINGS of the John Wanamaker Commercial Institute in 1896 grew the American University of Trade and Applied Commerce. Chartered by the Commonwealth of Pennsylvania on December 10, 1908, its purpose was

> ...to enable the students while earning a livelihood to obtain by textbooks, lectures, and by the school of daily opportunity, such a practical and technical education in the arts and sciences of commerce and trade that they may be better equipped to fill honorable positions in life and thereby increase their personal earning power. [5]

This school of practical learning was located on the eighth floor of the Philadelphia store. In addition to a variety of classrooms, there was an auditorium seating 1200 and a stage seating 700 more.

Writing to a friend who congratulated him for this endeavor, Wanamaker said, "It is one thing to build a ship, but it is much more important to train people to sail the ship." Because he did not have a formal education beyond grammar school, Wanamaker delighted in providing an opportunity for education to others. He explained:

> It was to recover what they had lost by leaving school early to come into the ranks of the wage-earner to help the mother,

to help little children, to help keep the home.[6]

Once the students reached the age of twenty-one, they were no longer required to attend the Institute but had the option of enrolling in post-graduate courses. They also, at that time, became full-fledged employees of the store and were qualified to engage in the activities of the Meadowbrook or Millrose Athletic Associations, the former for the Philadelphia employees and the latter for those in the New York store.

Both of these clubs, initially limited to Wanamaker employees, opened membership to the public and developed an international reputation for the athletic records won by its members in field and track. The Wanamaker Millrose Games, held each year in New York since 1908, are often referred to as the world's most prestigious indoor track and field meet. It is the oldest invitational indoor meet and the second oldest continuing event in the long history of Madison Square Garden. Once again it is noted that the influence of Wanamaker has continued in various community and public service endeavors long after his death.

The John Wanamaker Commercial Institute, in its educational endeavors, has had no equal in the history of storekeeping. Though it is difficult to ascertain the total number of boys and girls who attended the Institute, it is known that more than 7500 attended during the first fifteen years and many more attended in the years that followed.

POST NOTES

AFTER WORLD WAR I, the veterans of the two stores organized themselves into American Legion Posts 413 (New York) and 661 (Philadelphia). They were actively engaged in Legion events both locally and nationally and their marching band received wide acclaim. Though the New York Post no longer exists, members of the John Wanamaker Post 661 in Philadelphia still pay tribute to their fallen comrades twice each year as they place a wreath by the gold star in the Philadelphia store Grand Court on Memorial Day and Veteran's Day.

Camp Wanamaker at Island Heights was made available to the U.S. Army during World War II and used as a base recreational area and lookout post. Presently, the Island Heights Historical Society is involved in a restoration project of the two buildings on this six-and-a half acre site that carries such remarkable history.

A Pioneer in Business

WHENEVER MENTION IS MADE of the early pioneers of America, one immediately visualizes the frontier woodsmen and their families crossing the great plains in covered wagons seeking to establish a new way of life. Possessing an adventuresome spirit and a willingness to face difficult obstacles, they looked for a land that would satisfy their dreams. They hoped for a better world.

But there are other pioneers opening new territory in the fields of science, industry, education, agriculture and business. New frontiers will always be found and old ones challenged as long as the spirit of courage, hope and determination remains in the human heart.

Alfred Lord Tennyson understood the pioneer spirit and the challenge of life as he wrote in *Ulysses*:

> Tis not too late to seek an newer world. Push off...Strong in will...To strive, to seek, to find, and not to yield. [1]

Such was the determination and will of John Wanamaker: to find new and better ways to conduct mercantile trade in a rapidly growing nation. Never satisfied with past accomplishments and refusing to be bound by tradition, he became a pioneer in business by introducing his four cardinal points:

Full Guarantee of Goods,
One Price for All,
Returnable Goods, and
Money Refundable.

It was the first of many innovations that characterized his business and personal life-style. One of the publications distributed by the store for many years listed innovations begun at Wanamakers. A few of them are given here so that the reader may more fully appreciate the foundations Wanamaker laid, foundations upon which later generations have built.

THE WANAMAKER FIRSTS

1876	First restaurant in any general store.
	First to send buyers to study foreign markets.
1877	First store to present Paris and Berlin fashions in America.
1878	First store lighted by electricity.
	First to inaugurate the now famous "White Sales."
	First to set aside a special day for "The Little Fellows."
1879	First full-page newspaper advertisement.
	First store to use the telephone.
1880	First general store to institute shoe-repairing. (By 1924, the store employed thirty-two cobblers.)
	Use of pneumatic-tubes to carry money to the cashier's desk.
	Inauguration of the popular "Children's Day."
	Beginning of Queen Mary Laboratories, which made perfumes, face creams, tonics, soaps, etc.
1881	Establishment of Wanamaker Insurance Association for employees.
	Introduction of daily weather forecasts in the store's newspaper advertisements.
	Beginning of Wanamaker Art Gallery.
	First store to manufacture its own hair mattresses.
1882	Elevators first installed in the store.
1885	Opening of Market Street Laundry. (Pick-up and delivery of laundry was combined with purchase deliveries.)
1887	Opening of Hotel Walton which provided accommodations for women employees.
1888	Founding of the First Penny Savings Bank.
1894	Inauguration of full-day closing on New Year's Day.
1896	First store to manufacture its own down quilts.
	Founding of the John Wanamaker Commercial Institute for the instruction of young boy and girl employees.

1897	Opening of Annie E. McDowell Library for use by employees.
	First store to institute profit-sharing plan for employees.
1900	First to provide two-weeks free summer vacation at seashore for young employees.
	Establishment of the first private telephone system in a store, with about twenty-five telephones.
1903	Inauguration of Students' Art Exhibition.
1904	First to mark accurate yardage on spools and indicate the number of hairpins in hairpin boxes.
	First United States exhibition of Radium, discovered in 1898.
1905	First to provide 24-hour telephone service for customers.
1907	Children's Christmas drawing contest.
1908	Chartering of the American University of Trade and Applied Commerce, located in the Philadelphia store.
1910	First issue of *Store and Home*, a fashion-and-mail-order magazine.
	Grand Army Day first celebrated in Egyptian Hall.
1911	President Taft dedicates new building.
	Crystal Tea Room opened; largest restaurant in any store.
	World's largest organ installed in store.
	First store to exhibit photographs of the coronation of King George V and Queen Mary.
1912	Wanamaker Marconi station on roof of New York store receives news of the Titanic disaster. Wanamaker's wireless operator, David Sarnoff, later became Chairman of the Radio Corporation of America.

John Wanamaker Commercial Institute Insignia

1913	First parcel-post package mailed in Philadelphia by John Wanamaker.
	First store to provide free parcel-post delivery to customers.
1915	Athletic field opened on roof of the Wanamaker store for use by employees.
1916	The Red, White and Blue Inc., is formed in the store, enabling employees to give cooperative service in time of public emergency and war.
1918	Public singing of Christmas carols began.
1919	$39 million dollars subscribed to U.S.Liberty bonds by and through the store.
	Leopold Stokowski led the Philadelphia Orchestra with M. Courboin, organist, in public concert in Grand Court.
	John Wanamaker Foundation organized for the benefit of employees, providing pensions, life insurance, cooperative savings and sick relief.
1920	John Wanamaker led the nation's businesses in lowering prices 20% after World War I.
	Postal permit #1 first issued in Philadelphia to John Wanamaker allowing a business to send pre-paid letters without regular stamps.
1922	First radio broadcast from Wanamaker store with the first ever transmission of organ music by radio—Wanamaker station WOO.

A Young Man Turns to God

"YOUR OLD SUPERINTENDENT GAVE HIS HEART AND LIFE to God at fifteen."
So wrote John Wanamaker, age 79, the superintendent of Bethany Sunday
School, in May, 1917, when illness kept him at home.

> I am hoarse today from a cold and without the voice to speak
> to you on Sunday, I fear,—yet I must give you in this way
> what I would have said.[1]

For sixty years he had led the Sunday School which he had started
with just twenty-seven boys and girls in a second-floor room over a cobbler's shop. It became the largest Sunday School in America with 5000
scholars in attendance each Sunday.

And now, once again, he was telling the story of his youth when he
gave his "heart and life" to God.

Walking home, down Broad Street in Philadelphia after working all
day, he heard singing in the Chamber's First Independent Church at
Broad and Sansom Streets. Attracted by the music, he entered the mid-
week prayer service and heard an elderly layman speak of his many years as
a follower of Christ. The old man declared that now he felt well-prepared
to die and meet his Maker. Such a testimony had no appeal to young
Wanamaker who was just beginning his life and wasn't thinking about
death, only the present.

Then another man, quite young, said that he had been a Christian
only a brief time but felt that being a Christian was all that a young man
could dream for. Wanamaker liked that and went to the minister after the
service to say, "Tonight I have given my heart and life to God."

That decision determined the character of his personal life and the
policies of his business ventures until the day he died. It compelled him to
suggest that his epitaph simply read "Servant of God."

Bethany Presbyterian Church
PHILADELPHIA, PENNSYLVANIA

Founded by John Wanamaker, 1858

THE STORY OF BETHANY PRESBYTERIAN CHURCH is almost as remarkable as the life and career of John Wanamaker himself. From its early beginnings with a small group of children on a Sunday afternoon in 1858, it grew to become the largest Sunday School in America in 1900 with 5098 pupils.

A BEEHIVE OF RELIGIOUS ACTIVITY

> I speak to you tonight, Dear Friends, everyone of the three thousand of you, with heartfelt pleasure.
>
> For thirty years I have been sitting in this Bethany boat, with my back to the future, pulling away at the oars—not always doing my best I regret to say, but thanks to the Kingly Pilot, the boat has been kept on its course, and, guided by His hand, is far upstream tonight with a happy company bound for the Holy City, the New Jerusalem coming soon from God out of heaven.
>
> The winds have been all favorable this past year. It was an extra good year. We had the usual fifty-two Sundays and an extra one thrown in for good measure. Many scholars were here every Sunday in the year and your old Superintendent has a good mark also for every one of the fifty-three Sundays. [1]

As he spoke these words, fifty-one year old John Wanamaker was celebrating another anniversary as superintendent in the Sunday School he had started with just twenty-seven children. The membership had grown to 2603 children and adults. "That's the best we have ever done, but not the best we can and will do," he said in 1889.

That same year he became the Postmaster General of the United States after campaigning for the election of Benjamin Harrison, Republican candidate for the Presidency of the United States. His business was booming at the Grand Depot as more and more departments with new merchandise, or "specialty shops," as he called them, were added. At the same time, the Grand Depot was undergoing reconstruction and expansion to accommodate the growing crowds of shoppers.

Yet these things did not interfere with the work of Bethany Sunday School, Wanamaker's first love. It must not be forgotten that three years before he began his first clothing store, he started the ministry of Bethany. He loved to recount that early experience:

> On one snowy winter afternoon, February 7, 1858, I went with Mr. F. H. Toland, one of the missionaries of the American Sunday School Union, to the second-story back room of a dwelling house on Pine Street, near twenty-third, to start a mission school. A few children gathered, but not to stay, for the place was invaded by gangs of rowdy young men called "killers" and "bouncers," who came with clubs and took possession of our quarters. We fled from the room with fear and trembling.
>
> I was then but a boy, and soon got over my scare, and as it was not easy to give up what I had started to do, that same afternoon we hunted until we found another room. It was on South Street, number 2135, and we took the refusal [option] that day. We returned during the week and rented the front second story room for five dollars per month, and on the Sabbath, the 14th of February 1858, we made the actual beginning of what was called the First Independent Mission. Some people could not get it into their heads what Independent meant. We had to change the name and we next called it Chambers Mission School and it finally settled to Bethany Mission School.
>
> The first session gathered twenty-seven children and two women [his sister, Mary and her friend, Mary Brown, later to become his wife] besides Mr. Toland and myself as

teachers. Benches we had none, and the shoemaker landlord found in his cellar some old boards and bricks, on which we sat and said our first lessons together. From the school windows we looked out over fields. Not a house, save one, was then built below South Street all the way to the Baltimore Railroad. It was a long stretch of brick ponds and brickyards, ash heaps and the like, such as are always found in the suburbs of a great city. It was the playground of "Schuylkill Rangers," who at that time held sway and were the terror of the southeast section of the city.

Sabbath after Sabbath more and more children came until we had no more room. We then rented an adjoining room, and filled it, piled the children on the staircase, and then added a third room downstairs. [2]

Wanamaker spoke with a mixture of gratitude and pride. By July, when the Sunday School outgrew the small building, a tent was erected. Mothers of the children had picked up old sails from the sailing ships that docked at the foot of South Street and had sewn them together to make the tent. The tent had seats for nearly 500, but upwards of 1000 could gather in and around the tent within hearing range of the teacher's voice. During August and September fifty-one services were held in the tent.

By October a lot on the north side of South Street, west of Twenty-first Street, was purchased from Mr. R. Dunning for a new building. They laid the cornerstone for Bethany Chapel on October 18th. In the cornerstone were deposited "the Charter of Bethany Mission, with the names of the Board of Trustees, the Building Committee, the Superintendent of the School and Teachers [Wanamaker], the President and Cabinet of the United States, the Judges of the Supreme Court of the United States, the Governor of Pennsylvania, the Mayor of Philadelphia, copies of many religious papers, journals, hymns and other publications." This was not just another passing event. Young Wanamaker had every expectation that a great and mighty work of God was about to happen.

Prevented by cold weather from meeting in the tent while the new building was under construction, the classes met at first in the railroad shed of the Lombard and South Street Railway and then at the public schoolhouse on Twenty-third Street above Lombard. Then, on January 27, 1859, just a year from the date of the first class meeting, the opening dedication service was held in the new building measuring 40 x 60 feet.

The School was active all day Sunday with classes in the morning and afternoon and preaching services in the evening. Neighboring ministers volunteered to preach as needed, including Rev. Dr. John Chambers who had been instrumental in Wanamaker's early steps of faith.

Many years later at the testimonial luncheon given by his business associates and friends honoring his sixty years in business, Wanamaker said, "I have never forgotten the Prayer Meeting in the old John Chambers Lecture Room, which I attended as a boy...."[3]

While walking home from work one evening, Wanamaker had heard singing as he passed Chamber's Church on the corner of Broad and Sansom Streets. Upon entering, he heard an old man tell how he was prepared to die - knowing Christ. Wanamaker commented at the luncheon that since he was so young, he had not been thinking about death, but about life. A young man nearer Wanamaker's age told how wonderful it was to be a Christian as he looked forward to a long life ahead of him. Impressed by the thought, Wanamaker waited after the service until everyone else had gone and then spoke to the minister, "Tonight I have decided to give my life to God." He was fifteen years old.

He continued attending Chamber's church, finding every opportunity he could to put his faith into practice. When he was only sixteen, he was elected assistant librarian of the Sabbath School. At eighteen he was elected a teacher and also became the secretary of the Teachers Association,

The Reverend Dr. John Chambers

serving in that capacity until he was twenty-one. By that time the Bethany Mission, an outgrowth of Chambers Church, demanded all the time that Wanamaker could find after his long day's employment at Philadelphia's Y.M.C.A. As superintendent at Bethany, he enlisted the cooperation of clergy and lay-people alike in establishing a church "where all shall come and worship...that it shall be free and independent, open for all of every denomination."

Though in later years Wanamaker became a staunch Presbyterian in both the local Presbytery and the national General Assembly, his early years of religious fervor were pursued as an independent. This was a characteristic of his business life as well.

At the close of the second year at Bethany Mission, a comprehensive and optimistic report was given in November 1859 announcing the success of the venture.

> ...Since we entered this field of labor, many precious souls have been brought into the Church through the humblest instrumentalities which God has so kindly blest. Seventeen persons have united with the First Independent Church, who are gleanings from our mission field, and a number of others have been led into a knowledge of the truth as it is in Christ, who have joined themselves to other branches of the family of the Saviour....Though we rejoice and thank God for what has been done, yet the usefulness of this enterprise could be extended ten-fold. [4]

Clearly the report was written by Wanamaker, because it contains the verbal expressions and optimism characteristic of him throughout life.

Although Wanamaker withdrew from the Chambers Church at this time and became identified solely with Bethany, he never forgot the influence of his pastor, Dr. John Chambers, nor the roots of his simple faith and service begun in "the Mother Church."

Bethany Chapel was not the only product of the missionary concern of the Chambers Church. The church also strongly supported the Y.M.C.A., known in the beginning as the Young Men's Christian Association, with emphasis upon the word "Christian." From 1858 to 1861, Wanamaker was employed as Secretary of this fledgling organization with an annual salary of $1000, a large sum in those days.

Like the church, the Y.M.C.A. was concerned about the wayward youth of the city, many of whom had come from their farming homes to find a new and successful way of life. Lacking moral influences or wholesome examples, the youth were prime targets for the immoral, corrupt and evil influences that accompany anonymity in large cities. With the encouragement of Dr. Chambers, Wanamaker, and his mentor, George H. Stuart, the Y.M.C.A. endeavored to strengthen existing Sunday Schools and to establish others. It is not surprising then that as Wanamaker challenged others to begin new schools, he would also set an example by starting one himself. Moreover, his Bethany set the pace and always kept a step or more ahead of the others.

Evangelism was a primary purpose of the Y.M.C.A. and teaching the Bible seemed to be one of the best ways to accomplish this. As the Y.M.C.A. Secretary taught the Bible, he constantly read and studied it and listened to great preachers. A deepening of his faith was bound to occur. In his diary on January 1, 1860 he revealed his innermost feelings, "I desire to herein make record of the doings of each day. Oh that I may redeem the time."

After attending church that same day, where the minister preached from the text, "This year thou shalt die," Wanamaker wrote, "O Lord, may I live in readiness." During that afternoon, he visited the Lutheran and German Reformed Sabbath School and the Union Prayer Meeting. At bedtime he wrote in his diary, "I long to be like Jesus." It was the theme of his life.[5]

As friends observed Wanamaker, some believed that he would become a minister. For three years he considered all possibilities and finally chose a career in business, with a corresponding life-long commitment to the Sunday School he loved so much. To him this decision offered the best of two worlds. Success in one or the other was not sufficient; he would set new standards and reach new heights in both.

As Bethany Mission grew steadily in numbers and activities, it became apparent that a more formal organization was needed. On September 21, 1865, Bethany Presbyterian Church was granted a charter by the court of Common Pleas of the City and County of Philadelphia. Subsequently the Presbytery of Philadelphia approved the organization of the church on October 13 with Rev. Samuel T. Lowrie as pastor of twenty charter members and one elder - John Wanamaker. In 1867 the name of the mission was changed to Bethany Memorial Presbyterian Church.

The church purchased land on the southeast corner of Twenty-second and Shippen Streets [now Bainbridge] for the construction of a church building, which was officially dedicated on the thirteenth of February 1868. Dr. Lowrie resigned in 1869 and was succeeded by Rev. J.R. Miller, D.D., who became the best of friends with Wanamaker. When these two men combined their talents, resources and goals, there seemed to be no limit for the growth in attendance and activities in both the Sunday School and the church. In 1874 the addition of a second building increased seating to 4820. One organization after another was established to meet the needs and interests of the congregants.

THE BETHANY BROTHERHOOD

THE BETHANY BROTHERHOOD was organized in 1890, when Wanamaker was Postmaster General, "to promote Christ's kingdom especially among men, and for their spiritual, social and mental improvement." Officially, it was a branch of the Brotherhood of Andrew and Philip, an organization founded in Reading, Pennsylvania. The Sunday morning gathering of men included talks, testimonies, prayers and singing, followed by a study of the

Bethany Presbyterian Church, Philadelphia (John Wanamaker, founder)

Bible. All this preceded the regular Sunday morning worship hour and afternoon Sunday School.

Well-organized, with elected officers, a variety of committees and a men's chorus to spread the Kingdom through song, the Brotherhood was open to any man promising to abide by two rules:

RULE OF PRAYER; to pray daily for the spread of Christ's kingdom among men, and for God's blessing upon the labors of the Brotherhood;

RULE OF SERVICE; to make an earnest effort to bring at least one man or one boy within the hearing of the Gospel of Jesus Christ as set forth in the service of the church. 6

Within ten years there were more than 900 men in attendance each Sunday. Believing that the men needed a meeting place of their own, Wanamaker built The Bethany Brotherhood House in 1900 on South Street, west of Twenty-first Street. This was the exact location where Wanamaker had started Bethany Sunday School above the cobbler's shop in 1858. The cost of the new building was $32,000. 7

In addition to a reading room on the ground floor, there was space for the men to play checkers, chess, shuffleboard, billiards and other table games. An auditorium seating 700 was located on the second floor, and a dining room and kitchen on the third. For those who wanted to relax in the sun, Wanamaker built a roof garden equipped with lounge chairs and tables. A few years later a swimming pool with showers and lockers was added. Wanamaker chose his good friend Thomas T. Horney, superintendent of The Friendly Inn, to oversee the work of The Brotherhood.

Next door to The Brotherhood Building at 2122-2127 South Street, Wanamaker built a two-story library, fully furnished and equipped with stacks for 15,000 books. He paid the cost of heat, electricity, janitorial services, a secretary and an assistant. In later years it was given to the City of Philadelphia and became The John Wanamaker Branch of the Free Library of the City of Philadelphia. It remained open until 1932, when Mr. Wanamaker's estate was settled.

Despite the numerous demands made on his time by his business, his civic and political associations, and his membership in a variety of organizations, Wanamaker always had time for the men of The Brotherhood. Their needs were his concerns. If one of them could not afford a hospital stay, he paid the bill. He sent letters, notes and postcards to those who were ill or out of work. When he had to be away on business or on vacation, he sent each member a card with an individualized message. From Germany in 1906, he wrote his son;

> I am laboring to break the back of the self-imposed duty of the man's [sic] postal cards. I have done about 400 and have yet 850 to do. The fitting of the cards to the men takes much time and the writing is more difficult this third year. I can only do about 15 an hour. They have to be addressed and my message written on the face, and I must do it all myself. Dr. Dickey offers to help, but that will not do. [8]

Teaching each Sunday from Paul's *Epistle to the Romans*, Wanamaker challenged the men of The Brotherhood to memorize the Bible verses of each week's lesson. To honor the men who succeeded, he organized yet another group called "The Roman Legion," inducted them in a special gathering at his country estate, Lindenhurst, and challenged others to follow their example.

Another Wanamaker innovation, The Brotherhood Yearly Savings and Loan Club, stated as its purpose:

> ...to present an opportunity for any man, woman or child to lay by during the year in weekly payments, small sums of money from 10 cents per week up. [9]

Money deposited throughout the year was returned just before Christmas. Basically, Wanamaker introduced what banks later called "The Christmas Club." A major difference however, was the ability of the members to borrow on their deposits throughout the year. All funds were deposited by the treasurer in the First Penny Savings Bank, which Wanamaker began in 1888 at Bethany, with the church janitor as its first teller. An account could be opened with just one penny. The Bank continued to grow with a main office and branch until it was absorbed by the Western Savings Fund Society of Philadelphia in 1934.

The Ladies' Auxiliary to the Brotherhood was comprised of nearly a hundred women in 1904. In addition to their regular meetings, the women conducted fairs and various entertainment and social gatherings all in the spirit of "benevolence and Christian usefulness."

The significance of The Brotherhood caught the attention of a nearby Roman Catholic church that sent "two priests and two laymen who spent much time studying the Brotherhood House with a view to adapting a plan in connection with their work."

During World War I, The Brotherhood Building was opened to all military personnel and provided meaningful opportunities for wholesome fellowship as well as a bed for 15 cents and breakfast for just 10 cents.

Wanamaker believed strongly in the mission and purpose of The Brotherhood. Toward the end of his life he looked back at its influence in changing many men's lives for good and said:

> On the Old Bethany Farm when 22nd and Bainbridge was all lots, we found a splendid spring that became the Brotherhood Well. Hundreds of men in the past 25 years drank from that well. Each man pumped up from its depths, knowledge and refreshing strength sent down to the well direct from the Bible rivers, whose source is God's Heaven. Somehow the men prospered as long as they camped by The Brotherhood Well....There is still enough and to spare, where they received their first blessing at the same old well, clear and sweet and satisfying for heart and soul in life and in death. [10]

EVANGELISM AND THE SOCIAL GOSPEL COMBINED

BETHANY WAS A FORERUNNER of "The Social Gospel" in the finest meaning of that term. Without question, the foundation upon which the ministry was built was a dynamic, theologically conservative interpretation of the Bible. Evangelism, or as Wanamaker referred to it, "receiving the Saviour," was foremost and first in the work. Late on a cold snowy March night, he wrote to the members of his Sunday School class, "If you are not saved, my dear Friend, flee to the merciful Saviour as you would fly into this warm room tonight out of the cold streets and the drifting snow." Beyond soul-winning, the Gospel message carried an implied commitment to meet people's daily needs in order to make life better, more enjoyable and more fulfilling.

As the church expanded its community services, Wanamaker bought most of the properties that surrounded Bethany to house the various ministries, as well as the pastors, assistant ministers, and deaconesses.

The Bethany Dispensary, located across the street from the church, started in 1891 and provided medical and surgical clinics, a dental clinic and an eye, ear, nose and throat clinic. In one year alone, 1913, it treated 8,337 patients.[11] The clinic was open at stated hours with physicians and nurses always in attendance.

In the first year of The Bethany Home and Day Nursery, 1891, 3500 children took advantage of the free kindergarten offered by Wanamaker. Located in the same block at 2139-2141 Bainbridge Street was a sick-diet kitchen, where thousands of kettles of beef broth and tea and many glasses of jelly were prepared for the ill and the infirmed. Named the Bethany Deaconess's Society in 1894, it helped hundreds of women find jobs through its employment bureau. Other women comprised a sewing bureau and made clothes for the needy.

ANNIVERSARIES, SPECIAL DAYS AND SOUVENIRS AT BETHANY

AMONG THE REASONS FOR THE AMAZING GROWTH of Bethany Sunday School was the emphasis that Wanamaker placed upon the celebration of anniversaries and other special days. Not one to limit celebrations to the fifth, the tenth or the twenty-fifth, Wanamaker felt that every year was an occasion to mark progress and to set new goals. It was a time of festive rejoicing. On one such day he prayed:

> Eternal Father, God of all time, we praise thee for this anniversary Sunday, thanking thee that thou hast put this house over our lives. We praise thee for a holy book and a holy day in which to study it. [12]

On each anniversary of the Sunday School all students in attendance received a special souvenir. In 1867 it was a colorful printed card, an "anniversary keepsake" with a Bible verse "Lord be thou my Helper," Psalm 30:10. In 1911 after attending the coronation of King George V, in London, Wanamaker returned with Royal Doulton China cups, imprinted with the pictures of the King and Queen, for each pupil. In 1920 it was a large photographic collage of the pictures of the nursery class children placed around the portrait of Wanamaker. At other times it was a candy dish, or books like Mrs. Osgood's *Little Canary* given on the thirty-third anniversary in 1891, and *Black Beauty* by A. Sewell in 1898.

A self-taught man who loved books, Wanamaker helped his pupils develop good reading habits by giving them books that many of them could not afford to buy. Some of the books had just been published, some were religious; others were classics, like *Twice Told Tales* by Nathaniel Hawthorne. When Sunday School picnics were held at Lindenhurst, his country home in Jenkintown, he gave a souvenir book as a memento of "their day in the woods."

In addition to anniversary Sundays, Wanamaker also highlighted Children's Day, Mother's Day, and patriotic days. He inaugurated Old Folk's Day at Bethany in recognition of his many long-time friendships established at the church. He provided free transportation for the old folks and a luncheon tendered in their honor. Long before others thought of large-print books for the elderly, Wanamaker gave the old folks a large-print copy of the "Psalms," which he ordered while he was in England.

AN ORDER OF WORSHIP

WANAMAKER INTRODUCED AN ORDER OF WORSHIP to the Sunday School movement and printed it for distribution each week. It was further evidence of his organizational skill and of his insistence that everything have purpose and order. Sunday School was not simply a time for fellowship, but for worship and instruction as well.

As superintendent, he began each session by reading a Bible verse to which the pupils responded with another verse. The singing of hymns accompanied by organ, piano and a large orchestra preceded the reading of the lesson text and prayer. Then the teachers instructed their classes in the lesson of the day. Specially designed horseshoe-shaped benches, one for each class, filled up every inch of space in the large room. Each bench seated ten students facing the teacher, the class secretary and the class visitor. After the lesson study by the class teachers, the Superintendent summarized the lesson in his own unique manner with interesting personal illustrations and stories.

Each week's order of worship was different. No one could be too sure what the Superintendent had planned next.

Absentees from the school were noted each Sunday and were visited before the week was out. It was the Wanamaker way to show how important everyone was at Bethany Sunday School.

John Wanamaker and Bethany Sunday School children

An attendance report given to the Superintendent before the close of the hour included a comparison with the preceding year's attendance as well as the number of visitors for the day. This procedure noted progress in Wanamaker's store and it would serve the Sunday School just as well.

Despite the increasing demands made upon Wanamaker's life in business, in local and national politics, and in numerous organizations which solicited his involvement, he never lost personal and individual contact with Bethany people. They were his friends—each one of them. With pride he claimed to know the names of about 4,000 people at the church, as well as their family relationships, their business or work. He loved people and wanted them to know that his interest in them was sincere. When they were sick, he visited them. When they needed encouragement or comfort, he wrote them a note. In later years, when he dictated correspondence to his secretary at the store, business letters were interspersed with letters sent to Bethany friends, for they were always on his mind.

THE BIBLE AT BETHANY

AS ONE READS THE HISTORY OF BETHANY and the personal involvement of John Wanamaker, it would be easy to conclude that the plans, programs and strategies he devised were the reasons for its success. Such a conclusion fails to take into consideration the central message of the school—the message of the Bible—which Wanamaker steadfastly proclaimed.

As a boy he had bought a small red-leather Bible from his teacher, Mr. Hurlock. Referring to its importance, when he was eighty years of age, he said that it was the biggest purchase that he had ever made. He lived by it; he taught it to others; and he believed in its importance for life and death. He prayed:

> Let thy Book breathe and burn and bless, and in thy revelations to us today, make us strong and glad and grow a great hope in our souls of the Everlasting Day, where no cloud, no death, no grave will shadow over us—but where victory will reign eternally. Amen. [13]

Wanamaker called the Bible "the Book of Truth," "the Gate of Mercy," and "the Foundation of Life." In teaching it, he taught his students about Jesus and prayed for them:

> We will make heart-room for Jesus, Thy Son, the name to sinners most dear. We live in the grace of His redeeming love and our only hope is the finished salvation of Calvary. Empty-handed, full of sin; sad of heart and conscious of aggravated wickedness, we cast ourselves at thy feet, O Christ. God be merciful to me a sinner. [14]

Few people knew the Bible as well as Wanamaker. Early each morning he read it at the breakfast table with family members present or sometimes with just a servant. It was the deep, still, small voice of God that opened the eyes of faith. He said:

> Whether or not we have anything else for breakfast in our house we have a text. This morning our text was: "Keep thy foot when thou goest to the House of God, and be more ready to hear than to give the sacrifice of fools." Ecclesiastes 5:1. [15]

WANAMAKER THE EVANGELIST

THOUGH WANAMAKER WAS A FRIEND to those of other faiths, he never apologized for being an evangelist in his own. He encouraged other Christians to reach out and tell of Christ's redeeming love. He challenged them by saying:

> If you once have the joy and sweet pleasure of bringing one soul to Christ, you will be hungry to get to another. Do not argue, do not be rebuffed, be patient and gentle and keep on with a prayer in your heart and drop a good word here and there as you go along. Oh, what a pleasure it will be to you to have a newborn soul beside you at the next Supper of the Lord. [16]

When Baron Shibusawa of Japan visited Philadelphia, the distinguished financier was the guest of honor at Bethany. A special order of worship for the day included the Bible verse, "For God so loved the world that He gave His only begotten Son, that whosoever believes in Him shall not perish, but have everlasting life." In presenting a Japanese Bible to the Baron, Wanamaker said, "There is a Living Man in this Book—that Christ is not dead. He was dead...and is living."[17]

Nearing the end of his life, he wrote in his diary of the meaning of his church and Sunday School work:

> Is Bethany the glory or tragedy of my life? Those Bethany Sundays are precious pearls making up the necklace

of years....I have always been happy in Bethany. It was the earliest habit I formed. It has been a blessing. Why people think my Bethany work is either virtue or prose, I can't imagine. I have always just liked it, and there isn't anything else, not business certainly, that I have just always liked and have gotten satisfactions and blessings, not worry, out of. [18]

JOHN CHAMBERS MEMORIAL PRESBYTERIAN CHURCH

BETHANY WAS ONE OF THE FIRST to establish branch churches remaining under the supervision and control of the mother church.

It began in an unusual way. On January 26, 1897 a devastating fire in Philadelphia destroyed most of the stores and buildings on the north side of Market Street between Thirteenth and Juniper, directly across from John Wanamaker's store on the south side. As flaming debris fell upon his wood-constructed building, employees fought frantically to save the store, passing buckets of water to one another. Though the six-story clock tower on the corner was destroyed and damage to other parts of the building amounted to $100,000, Wanamaker thanked God that the business was spared and promised to build another church as a thank-offering.[19]

Bethany Church had already established a mission in a tent at Grays Ferry Road near Carpenter Street on July 9, 1885. Wanamaker also owned a large plot of ground at Twenty-eighth and Morris Streets in an area where new homes were being built. Despite strong opposition from two neighboring Presbyterian churches, Wanamaker, the senior elder at Bethany, broke ground for the Bethany Memorial Chapel—his thank offering—in the spring of 1901. The cornerstone was laid on August 10. Following a week of special dedication services each evening, John Wanamaker handed the keys of the new church to the Chairman of the Board of Trustees on Sunday morning, October 26, 1902. He called it "the New House of the Lord" and "the Church of the Love of God."

Many members of Bethany, having moved into new homes in South Philadelphia, found it more convenient to worship closer to home. They transferred their membership to the new church, ultimately called the "John Chambers Memorial Presbyterian Church," after Wanamaker's spiritual mentor. Many others in the neighborhood also joined.

With a large 700-seat auditorium, a gymnasium, shower baths, dining room, kitchen, classrooms, a public reading room, and an adjoining ball field for the youth, the church endeavored to serve the South Philadelphia community with a variety of ministries. The Men's Friendly Union, founded in this church in 1911 by Wanamaker, was similar to the Brotherhood at Bethany. The Union's annual highlight was the Lincoln's Day Dinner, attended by many civic leaders and distinguished guests. Musical events and athletic contests attracted numerous young people, who were always a primary concern to Wanamaker.

BETHANY TEMPLE PRESBYTERIAN CHURCH

JUST AS SOME OF THE CITY'S POPULATION were moving south of Bethany, so others were crossing the Schuylkill River and building new homes in West Philadelphia. Bethany Church followed this movement with evangelistic concern. In February 1906 the Presbytery of Philadelphia organized Bethany Temple Presbyterian Church as another branch of Bethany. The church building was erected on a lot owned by John Wanamaker and once used as a stable area for his delivery wagons and horses. It was bounded by Fifty-third, Fifty-fourth, Spruce and Irving Streets.

During the preceding summer Wanamaker had erected a tent nearby his old barn for a series of meetings which he sponsored in cooperation with the Evangelistic Committee of the Philadelphia Presbytery. Services continued during the fall and winter months in a nearby hall until a temporary auditorium was completed at the tent site. By September 1906, 563 people were enrolled in the Sunday School, and in less than three years, the congregation had grown so rapidly that a permanent church building was constructed with a seating capacity of 1000 and plans for a balcony to accommodate several hundred more.

Like Bethany and the John Chambers Church, Bethany Temple conducted activities for all ages. In addition to the Sunday School classes and regular worship services, musical organizations of choirs and orchestra, women's ministries, sewing classes and the ushers association all provided opportunities for everyone to become involved. When the new educational building was added, it also contained a fully equipped gymnasium.

It is interesting to note that John Wanamaker organized the three churches into a collegiate relationship in which each congregation had its own ruling body of elected elders while all the elders formed a single

John Chambers Presbyterian Church, Twenty-eighth and Morris Streets, Philadelphia

Bethany Temple Presbyterian Church, Fifty-third and Spruce Streets, Philadelphia, 1906-69

"Collegiate Session" having oversight and final authority. A genius in organization and management, he founded a system where each church group was able to benefit from the combined strength and wisdom of the others. In 1911 his plan received the approval of the Philadelphia Presbytery, and Bethany Memorial Church was renamed Bethany Collegiate Presbyterian Church.

In this collegiate relationship the three churches also had the benefit of Wanamaker's name and personal involvement in their individual ministries. Without question, he was able to draw crowds of people wherever he was present. He was the inspirational leader for all three churches, three pastors, sixty elders, and all members in the congregations. The collegiate relationship continued until after Wanamaker's death in 1922.

Because of continued growth and the membership of Bethany Temple—the largest Presbyterian church in the Philadelphia area with 2600 members in 1926 [20]—a most amicable plan of separation occurred in that year. The Temple was given total independence from the collegiate relationship and was organized as a separate congregation. Bethany and the John Chambers Church continued their collegiate relationship for thirty-six more years.

In 1948 Bethany, the mother church, followed its membership to the suburbs relocating in Havertown, Pennsylvania, at Township Line and Concord Avenue, and continues as the Bethany Collegiate Presbyterian Church. The groundbreaking ceremony was held on May 16, with the daughter of John Wanamaker, Mrs. Barclay H. Warburton, participating. Dedication of the new building was held on September 18, 1949. The expansive church buildings and facilities at Twenty-second and Bainbridge Streets were sold to the Church of the Lord Jesus Christ of the Apostolic Faith. A few years later the church building was destroyed by fire.

In 1962 the John Chambers Memorial Church became a separate congregation and continues as such to this day. Among its most interesting historical memorabilia is the Bible used by John Wanamaker during the 1875-1876 Moody and Sankey revival meetings in Philadelphia, when Wanamaker served on the sponsoring committee. Hanging in the chancel of the church is a large 6'x 9' oil painting, "Jesus Healing a Blind Man," by Alfred Dabat, a gift of Wanamaker.

The John Wanamaker Memorial Tower and Church Spire of the Bethany Collegiate Presbyterian Church in Havertown recognizes its founder and also displays the original church pew that he and his wife occupied for more than sixty years. A nearby wall plaque, relocated from

Bethany Collegiate Presbyterian Church, Township Line and Concord Avenue, Havertown, Pa.

the old church at Twenty-second and Bainbridge Streets, reads as follows:

In Loving Memory of
John Wanamaker
Founder
1838-1922
By reason of Him many went
away and believed on Jesus

The magnificent church sanctuary of the Bethany Temple Church at Fifty-third and Spruce Streets was destroyed by fire in 1960. Steadily declining membership led the congregation to merge with the Bethany Collegiate congregation in April, 1969. The undamaged educational building, redesigned to accommodate a sanctuary as well as classrooms, was sold to Zion Hill Baptist Church.

OTHER CHURCHES

MANY OTHER CHURCHES IN THE PHILADELPHIA AREA, such as St. Paul's Presbyterian Church on Baltimore Avenue, were recipients of Wanamaker's favors. He and his wife contributed funds for the purchase of pianos, organs, stained glass windows, pulpit furniture and altars in addition to building programs.

Their son, Rodman, followed in their footsteps and presented the beautiful "Lady Chapel" to St. Mark's Episcopal Church in Philadelphia in memory of his wife, Fernanda Henry, who is buried beneath it. An architectural gem, the work of John Notman, the chapel contains a veritable treasure of plate and vestments employed in worship services, centered about an unusual and costly solid silver altar. The altar illustrates the descent of the Holy Spirit at Pentecost, the Resurrection, and the Ascension of Christ. It is seven-feet long, three-feet high and two-feet deep and contains 144 separate hand-tooled four-inch figures of saints and scenes from the life of Mary, the mother of Jesus.

Rodman Wanamaker also gave an altar for the Washington Memorial Chapel in Valley Forge, Pennsylvania. It is made of a solid block of Indiana limestone weighing over ten tons. One of the stained-glass windows in the chapel was the gift of his father.

Though the churches claiming some relationship to the Wanamaker family are too numerous to mention here, reference must be made to the Grace Presbyterian Church in Jenkintown, Pennsylvania, near Lindenhurst, John Wanamaker's country home on Old York Road. In 1870 Wanamaker offered to pay for the construction of a building for the Sunday School his children often attended in a nearby rented building. Before it was completed, Hattie, his five-year old daughter died. From that moment on, Grace Chapel became a memorial to the daughter he loved so much. In May, 1881 the Presbytery of Philadelphia organized the chapel into Grace Presbyterian Church at York and Vista Roads.

In a recently found handwritten letter to the Abington Presbyterian Church, dated September 4, 1872, Wanamaker wrote:

> The blessing attending the work in the Jenkintown Sabbath School and the goodness of God to me, first led me to decide on building this house for Him, and the death of a precious child, once a member of and greatly interested in the "Lyceum School," decided me to erect a better building, which should be in memorial of our beloved child.
>
> In committing this house then to you as its future guardian, I would only request that it be kept free of debt and be solely used to preach and teach the simple gospel of our Lord and Saviour Jesus Christ....
>
> I have made it my prayer that the new chapel may be a place where such a ladder as that of Jacob of old shall rest, that prayers and praise shall be constantly ascending and the blessing of a covenant keeping God shall be continually descending upon a happy people.... [21]

Ninety years later, in 1962, Grace Presbyterian Church dedicated a new Wanamaker Chapel in which hangs "The Adoration of the Magi" by the sixteenth century Italian perfectionist Paolo Veronese, a painting once owned by Wanamaker. A nearby stained-glass window pictures John Wanamaker standing at a pulpit as though teaching his Sunday School class. The background depicts his life, showing Bethany Church, his large Philadelphia store building and the symbol of the Y.M.C.A.

Few individuals have had such a widespread influence upon the formation and early growth of so many churches as John Wanamaker, a devout layman and servant of his Lord. It is not surprising that he said,

If you find yourself beginning to love any pleasure
    better than your prayers,
Any book better than the Bible,
Any house better than the house of God.
Any table better than the Lord's table,
Or any person better than Christ,
Or any indulgence better than the Hope of Heaven,
Take Alarm! [22]

THE WEATHERVANE MESSAGE

You have heard about the old deacon that invited Mr. Spurgeon, the famous preacher of London, to come down to the country to see him. When the old man received Mr. Spurgeon, he walked him around and showed him the gardens and the barns.

Mr. Spurgeon saw the weathervane on the barn and said, "Why deacon, what is that up there?" The deacon said, "Spell it out; it spells 'God Is Love.'"

"Why Deacon," said Mr. Spurgeon, "You don't mean that God is as shifting as the wind?" The old Deacon with his sweet face said, "No, Mr. Spurgeon, I think that it means, which ever way the wind blows, God is Love."

John Wananaker
Commencement Address
Perkiomen School, 1902

Pious John

ALL WHO KNEW JOHN WANAMAKER became fully aware of his deep religious faith. It was as natural to him as breathing and was the foundation for the principles upon which he established his successful ventures of life.

Never did he think or act as though his religion were hidden in one pocket and the rest of life in another. It was not something that occasionally intertwined with the other parts of life nor a resource drawn upon in emergencies or used when convenient; rather, it was the fiber of his life. To him, life consisted of religious faith just as it consists of oxygen, water, flesh, bones, soul and spirit. To remove any of them would be to terminate life itself. Religion, or faith as he preferred to call it, was the *sine qua non* of life; its substance.

Though he had gained international reputation as a merchant, his religious interests were foremost and primary. He could not extricate himself from the consequences of his faithful living; nor did he want to. When a newspaper cartoonist caricatured him as "Pious John," he humbly took it not as ridicule but as a challenge to an earnest and sincere piety; a quality of life worth striving for.

When as a young man he was deeply engrossed in Sunday School work, tent meetings and personal evangelism, friends felt that he would become a minister. He knew that his mother, a devout woman, would have liked nothing better, and his grandfather had set an example in this vocation by serving as a part-time preacher. But when the day of decision arrived, young John chose his vocation in a non-emotional systematic manner which he described in his late seventies in the following words:

> I took an enormous sheet of brown paper and wrote down
> on it all the different things I thought I should like to be. I

remember it very clearly to this day. I put down architect, because I had always been interested in the making of buildings. I put down journalist and doctor and clergy-man—the latter a vocation which my mother was very anxious to have me take up. After several others which I do not recall, I wrote merchant. One by one I went over the list and after careful deliberation struck out various words for one reason or another. Finally, merchant was left and I turned my attention seriously to work. [1]

Once the decision was made, he committed his mind and energy to it. Obviously, it was the right choice for he so thoroughly enjoyed his work, became extremely successful in it, and never gave it up until he died in his eighty-fifth year. As a merchant he was as active in church and religious affairs as he could have been as a minister. His influence as a Christian in business reached far beyond the normal confines of the church and knew no bounds of organization, institution, creed or geography. In speaking to a friend, he said that though he had once considered the ministry as a vocation, he felt that he could accomplish even more along the same lines while being a merchant. Obviously he was right.

Wanamaker did not attend a theological seminary or pursue any formal religious education, but he was an avid student of the Bible. He quickly acquired an understanding of theology from his many ministerial friends and the reading of numerous books. Each week he listened to some of the best-known preachers and spent considerable time preparing Sunday School lessons which he taught to an ever-increasing number of students in his "Superintendent's Class" at Bethany.

A LIFE OF PRAYER

As a child he had heard his parents pray, but now prayer became a personal experience. His prayers revealed his own belief that God is real and loving. He prayed:

> Living and Loving God, God of Life and God of love,
> we worship Thee as our heart's only God. [2]

Found among his papers is a short prayer, handwritten in his diary of

1858 when he was but twenty years of age. It reads: "I long to be like Jesus." More than forty years later, in another diary he wrote:

> Lord God, Father, Son and Holy Ghost, I, on my knees once more, write and sign this surrender of my body and soul, inside and out, to Thee forever.
> Sunday, 12:30 noon
> Dec. 10, 1899 [3]

Though he did not write any theological treatises, his papers include hundreds of prayers—written on small scraps of notepaper or the backs of used envelopes—which he prepared each week for the opening worship services at the Sunday School. Following his death, many of his prayers were compiled into three books published by one of the pastors of his church, the Reverend Dr. A. Gordon MacLennan. The following excerpts show his heart and mind regarding some common religious themes.

The Trinity

"Eternal Father so pitiful; Eternal Christ so tender; Eternal Spirit so patient; heal and help and hold on to us with mighty love, full pardon, and an abounding grace. Amen."

"O Thou who art the Beginning and the End, who art all in all; we worship Thee as the Creator, Ruler, the Father, the Son and the Holy Ghost— there are not three Gods, but one including all."

Sin

"We are sinners. God be merciful unto us. We have had a festival of hunger and a dance of shame. We have had spasms of consciousness and went straight on in willful, stubborn disobedience. We tried to drown them in liquor and wrong doing; but we are determined not to play the devil's game any longer. Forgive our transgressions, Merciful Father, and put away our sins, for the sake of Him who bore our transgressions on the painful Cross."

Salvation

"O Thou who art the Shepherd and the Door, in whom all figures and symbols meet, help us not to stop at the doorway, but to enter in and be saved."

"Thou Blessed Son of God, our only Priest and Saviour, show us that thy forgiveness is greater than our guilt."

Resurrection

"In the name of our Risen Christ, Amen. Make us to know the power of the Lord's resurrection, for Thy glory."

Sabbath

"Almighty and Eternal God. We reverently thank Thee for the bright day of the week; for the curtain that veils the other days of the week, that we

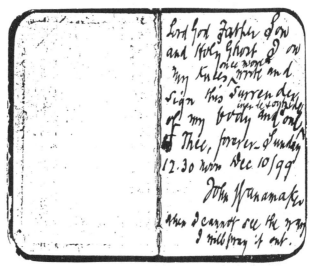

From John Wanamaker's diary: "Lord, God, Father, Son and Holy Ghost, I on my knees once more, write and sign this surrender of my body and soul, inside and outside, to Thee, forever. Sunday, 12:30 noon, December 10, 1899. John Wanamaker. When I cannot see the way, I will pray it out."

may find the Sabbath jewel. Make us glad in Thy day, and in Thy house. Refresh, elevate and enoble us."

"Our Father, Thou has given us fifty-two blessed Sundays in the year to be shining lamps to brighten our way."

Bible

"Let Thy book breathe and burn and bless. We have studied together, chapter after chapter, for years and years, but we have not finished school. We cannot lay down the Book of God which constantly throws new light on the Father and the world to come."

Death

"Though we are always dying, yet we cannot die, even though our flesh must fall into the grave. Death is the porch of immortality given to us by our Lord Jesus Christ and by His power our spirits shall rise to praise Him through endless years."

Jesus

"O Thou Son of Man, whose love is marked by five red wounds, hold our hearts steady and our feet firm and wait for us at the appointed Jerusalem on high."

"O Lord, hear thou the utterance of our thankfulness through Jesus our Saviour."
"We ask it in the name of the One who came not to be ministered unto, but to give his life a ransom for others."

"O Thou who didst put death under Thy feet and didst overcome the evil one, to whom shall we go with our sins and confessions and prayer, but unto Thee."

"We thank Thee for the gift of Jesus Christ, the most wondrous proof of Thy love, and for redemption through the precious blood which he so freely shed to atone for our guilt and to cleanse us from all sin."

"We are tenants with a short lease. We take air and sunshine and light to use brains and body and eyes and ears. Make us to remember that we must render our account to Thee as any servant does to his Master."

RELIGION AND BUSINESS

ALTHOUGH WANAMAKER WAS NEVER VIEWED AS A MODEST PERSON, he did not possess either the arrogance or vanity of some other successful business giants and philanthropists of his day. His personality was a refreshing mixture of rare individuality, unquestionable genius and unapologetic goodness. He was a very sincere religious man unashamed of his sectarian Protestant Christian beliefs. He believed the Bible to be the most vital book ever written—with a message both clear and demanding. In religion and theology he was a conservative; in business a liberal.

Believing that his store belonged to all the people, he never imposed his faith or doctrine upon his employees. In fact, he publicly stated:

> A man's or woman's nativity or creed is not made a condition for employment by our establishment, but only intelligence, integrity and capability. [4]

He did not refrain, however, from declaring his personal beliefs when appropriate. Christmas and Easter, in particular, were special times for him. They provided a unique opportunity for him to transform the Grand Court into a cathedral with enormous paintings of "Christ Before Pilate" and "Christ on the Cross." Customers and employees alike gathered to sing traditional Easter hymns and Christmas carols accompanied by the Great Organ and guest musicians. In one Christmas booklet he wrote:

> In all the coinage of days since the world began, no day ever equaled the birthday of Mary's son in the stable of the little inn at Bethlehem....Christmas is a Man born, not a sentiment. [5]

At Bethany Sunday School, leading a class of nearly a thousand students he said:

"Why I Go to Church"

Hon. John Wanamaker

You might just as pertinently inquire "Why do I eat?" or "Why do I sleep?"—because I find one is just as necessary to my well-being as the other.

I could eat well and sleep well, and yet be a very miserable man without the spiritual uplift that only comes from an attendance upon the Divine ordinances.

Then again, it is a great privilege to touch shoulders with the earnest Christian men who are also interested in promoting Christ's Kingdom upon earth.

For four years while Postmaster General under the Harrison administration, I traveled nearly 100,000 miles in order to be present each week at my own church.

I have made it the rule of my life to be in my regular place each Lord's day when in health and in the country, believing that Paul was inspired to write that we should not forsake the assembling of ourselves together.

I also believe that the temptations of every man are great, and unless he has more than the ordinary groundwork of honesty and faithfulness, he may be caught by the sudden wind of plausible opportunity and tumble over the precipice and be ruined.

We pray at the Cross, look upon the red blood which is a redeeming stream; we look at five wounds, five entrances into Thy love and Thy kingdom. Point out the One Saviour, the One Heaven, the One Truth and One Way. [6]

But in deference to employees who did not share his sectarian views, he refrained from religious sounding vocabulary in business communications and spoke of commonly desired virtues like fairness, decency, honesty, respect, cordiality and pleasantness, all of which he believed were the products of a genuine religious faith.

As a man who faced one day at a time with a sense of excitement and intrigue, it is not surprising that the favorite hymn of John Wanamaker was "Lead Kindly Light," written by Cardinal John Henry Newman:

Lead Kindly Light, amid the encircling gloom;
Lead thou me on!
The night is dark and I am far from home,
Lead thou me on!
Keep Thou my feet;
I do not ask to see the distant scene;
One step is enough for me. [7]

HIS FAVORITE BIBLE VERSE

WANAMAKER'S DAILY READING OF THE BIBLE was an inspiration to him in his business, community and church life. Frequently he quoted Bible verses in his public speeches as well as in his letters. When asked in 1898 by one correspondent about the Bible verse that gave him the most solid anchorage, he replied:

My favorite verse is John, 5th chapter, 24th verse, "Verily, verily, I say unto you, He that heareth my word and believeth on Him that sent Me, hath everlasting life and shall not come into condemnation, but is passed from death into life." [8]

A 33rd Degree Mason

As a humanitarian and a profound believer in the essential brotherhood of all humanity, John Wanamaker devoted his life to the service and good of others.

He belonged to numerous organizations of every sort in order to help them fulfill their goals. Whereas some people join clubs, churches and the like because of their need for identification with others, a desire to fill up idle hours, to find an outlet for service, or to make profitable business contacts, those things had already been taken care of in Wanamaker's life through his store and Bethany Church. He personally needed nothing more. But he fervently believed in the worthiness of the endeavors of others and lent his name and money to enhance their causes. It was his way of encouraging them to uphold high ideals and lofty purposes for the general welfare of society.

Hundreds of clubs, civic societies, religious and humanitarian organizations invited him to join. Many were willing to forego the usual prerequisites for membership if only he would consent to become a part of their group. It would be a boon for them just to list his name on their membership rolls.

Early in his life he declined most invitations, but in later years his memberships included several dozen organizations, not the least of which was the Masonic Order. He was nearly sixty years old when he was made a Mason at sight on March 30, 1898.

His becoming a Mason may have been a disturbing surprise to many of his evangelical minister friends who strongly opposed any secret fraternal organization. Wanamaker himself had often criticized such organizations as being undemocratic and a "breeding ground of intolerance." However, when once he observed the international breadth of Freemasonry and understood that he might be showing intolerance himself by remaining aloof from many of his friends who were Masons, he applied for membership.

In an interesting move, he and his good friend, Rabbi Joseph Krauskopf, were admitted at the same time to the first three degrees by the Grand Lodge of Pennsylvania. Shortly thereafter he joined the Friendship Lodge No. 400 at Jenkintown near his country home and became its Worshipful Master in just five years. Diligent and enthusiastic in whatever he undertook, he was crowned a 33rd Degree Mason in 1913 by the Supreme Council of the A.A. Scottish Rite.

Throughout his years as a member, right to the end of his life, he was particularly interested in the Library and Museum of the Grand Lodge of Pennsylvania. Appointed to the Library Committee in 1906, he later became chairman of the committee and also donated many valuable books and documents, the most notable being *The Sephar Torah*, an ancient Hebrew scroll of the Pentateuch, estimated to be 300 to 500 years old. Other gifts included an oil portrait of George Washington and a solid gold-plated invitation issued to President McKinley in 1901. Under his initiative the Masonic Museum was founded in 1908.

Always one to freely give souvenirs of important events or anniversaries at his store, his church or the lodge, he distributed a specially printed edition of Pastor Wagner's book, *A Simple Life*, to all in attendance when President Theodore Roosevelt visited the Pennsylvania Grand Lodge in Philadelphia in 1903. There was no relationship between the book and the visit; he simply used the occasion to share a book he personally enjoyed.

Frequently asked to speak at public ceremonies of historical significance, Wanamaker freely consented. His address at the laying of the cornerstone of the Odd Fellow's Orphanage in Philadelphia on September 4, 1911, reveals his respect and admiration for the Fraternity. He said:

> Free Masonry and the Odd Fellows make for good citizenship, enforcement of laws and true friendship...These orders are built upon the Bible and work with the Bible. They helped to prove the Bible....These fraternities do not form a church or take the place of a church, but they gather into their brotherhood men of all races, faces and places to practice the graces of true religion....I count it a privilege for a man to find the way into any place where liquors, profanity, gambling, indecent books, papers and speeches are excluded

and where he is brought face to face to be reverently taught
to think of the Word of God....The binding life of a lodge is
its altar upon which lies an open Bible. [1]

Two years before his death Wanamaker was made a member of the
American Supreme Council, an honor given to only a few. And now, more
than seventy years after his death, the Friendship Lodge in Jenkintown still
meets in the beautiful classic Doric-style Temple that Wanamaker built for
them in 1913, upon land he purchased for that purpose.

In the hallway leading to the large Lodge Room that can seat 350
hangs a full-length oil portrait of Wanamaker, a memorial to one who told
his son:

It is the best of life to impart ourselves to those in need and
find out that it is more blessed to give than to receive. [2]

Masonic Lodge Insignia

Postmaster General: John Wanamaker

IN BUSINESS AND RELIGION, John Wanamaker was always a leader, incapable of keeping lockstep with a political party, religious denomination or any other form of partisanship. Nevertheless, as long as the Republican Party held to his avowed principles of life, he remained a faithful and loyal worker and supporter.

Much of his political enthusiasm depended upon the particular individuals running for or holding office. He strongly believed in Abraham Lincoln and the ideals he espoused, as well as General Grant who became a friend and ordered his uniforms from Wanamaker.

Although he had been a major importer of foreign goods for many years, Wanamaker surprisingly supported the protectionist plank of the Republicans in the election year of 1888. His position may have been the result of an unwillingness to desert the party of Lincoln, which had brought about the unification of the nation, as well as his respect for the many thousands in the Grand Army of the Republic who had sacrificed their lives in the Civil War. He believed that reform of the Party from within was an endeavor worthy of his involvement and used the national prominence he was gaining toward that goal.

Moreover, Senator Quay, National Chairman of the Republican Party, needed the help of Wanamaker to enlist the support of wealthy businessmen to finance the election. Though an outspoken critic of Quay's corrupt handling of Pennsylvania's politics, Wanamaker nevertheless consented to serve the National Committee in creating an advisory board of businessmen responsible for raising funds and controlling their release. Typical of Wanamaker, he set up a procedure giving him ultimate influence over a small executive committee with full powers to disperse the funds received.

Business leaders, in favor of a high tariff on imports, responded with alacrity in contributing more than $200,000, the largest sum ever used in a political campaign up to that time. Wanamaker stated that he personally had given $10,000 to the campaign, no small contribution for an individual to make in those times. The Republicans won the election and placed Benjamin Harrison in the White House.

BENJAMIN HARRISON ELECTED PRESIDENT

A LAWYER IN INDIANA, Harrison was a man of impeccable character. Like Wanamaker, he, too, was a Sunday School teacher and an elder in the Presbyterian Church. Though the two had never met prior to the election, Harrison was a candidate that Wanamaker could support without reservation.

Harrison was fully aware of the part Wanamaker played in his election, and it seemed quite natural for the President-elect to summon Wanamaker to his Indianapolis office to discuss a possible Cabinet appointment. Both strongly believed in providential occurrences, but both also knew that political reward—called patronage—was the name of the game. How best, then, could Harrison and the Republican Party reward Wanamaker for helping to put the party back in power again after the Grover Cleveland—Democratic hiatus?

Wanamaker accepted Harrison's hand-written invitation with enthusiasm, even though Harrison had misspelled his name in it, not once, but twice. It seems humorous to us now, but it could have been seen as an inconsiderate affront to a man of prestige. Wanamaker easily rose above it, if for no other reason than for the unusual opportunity presented to him.

When they met, Harrison, like so many others before him and after, was immediately struck by the affable, quick-witted, sincere but strong-willed Wanamaker, just fifty years old. Here was a man with a sense of purpose not only for himself, but for the world as well. Wanamaker felt that life was to be lived honestly, justly, decently and enjoyably. And he lived this way himself as he labored for the rights of others.

WANAMAKER REWARDED

HARRISON MADE IT CLEAR: HE WANTED WANAMAKER to serve as Postmaster General. Wanamaker considered the offer to be more than an honor; it was a challenge to put the government on a sound businesslike track. Believing that it was an invitation to introduce proven business practices and ethical principles to the highest levels of the United States Government, he accepted the appointment. As in his department store, where he said "Put the customers first," so also as Postmaster General he intended to institute reforms and startling innovations in order to provide quality postal service for the public good.

Not everyone was happy about Harrison's choice. The Democrats blamed Wanamaker for their defeat, accusing him of buying votes in New York and other areas for Harrison, and now he, not the new President, became the focus of their attacks. In their minds, he certainly did not deserve the appointment; how could a simple "shopkeeper" qualify for a Cabinet position in the Federal Government. His formal education amounted to only a few years, and those before he reached his teens. He also was hardly known outside the Philadelphia area and then only in religious circles. Socially, his time was spent primarily in church and Sunday School or with preachers and evangelists.

Despite numerous unproven accusations that Wanamaker had bought his way into the Cabinet, he was not deterred from accepting the post. He moved to Washington after putting his large retail business in the hands of his eldest son Thomas and other trusted employees. Politically naive, he thought that the favorable reputation he had earned in thirty years of business would carry over into the political arena. He was wrong.

Joseph Pulitzer of the *New York World*, hoping to discredit him, conducted a most thorough investigation of his store practices, only to find the most favorable reports. Even accusations of the mistreatment of his employees, tax evasion and improper, if not illegal, business transactions proved to be incorrect. Political cartoonists had a field day with Wanamaker who was much easier to caricature than the President. It was also less risky for them to denounce a politically "unknown" individualist who seemed more intent on getting his own way than abiding by the rules of the system.

Considering himself a servant of the people, appointed by the President for the public good, Wanamaker set about his task: to efficiently and effectively reform the Post Office Department. Several significant changes occurred.

FRANK LESLIE'S
ILLUSTRATED
NEWSPAPER

Entered according to Act of Congress, in the year 1889, by Mrs. Frank Leslie, in the Office of the Librarian of Congress at Washington.—Entered at the Post office, New York, N. Y., as Second-class Matter.

No. 1,752.—Vol. LXVIII.]   NEW YORK—FOR THE WEEK ENDING APRIL 13, 1889.   [Price, 10 Cents. $4.00 Yearly. 13 Weeks, $1.00.

THE SUNDAY TALKS OF THE POSTMASTER-GENERAL.—HON. JOHN WANAMAKER ADDRESSING THE BETHANY SUNDAY-SCHOOL, PHILADELPHIA.

FROM A SKETCH BY F. ADAMS.—SEE PAGE 155.

DEVOTED TO A WORK ETHIC, he immediately replaced numerous Democratic postmasters whom he considered parasites, draining the lifeblood of a system that deserved quality performance at every level. Side-stepping the issue of civil service for the present, he appointed individuals whom he thought were better qualified and who were Republicans. Thus he further opened the door for patronage appointments. More criticism followed. Yet Wanamaker believed that his actions would be vindicated by the effectiveness of the service that resulted. After all, that had been his experience numerous times back in the City of Brotherly Love.

Impressed with the scope of his office, Wanamaker made certain that others would also appreciate the significance of the Post Office Department. In his first Report of the Postmaster General to the President in November 1889 he stated:

> To the Postmaster General is committed the management of the largest business concern in the world, consisting of a central establishment with almost 60,000 branches, and employing over 150,000 people....
>
> The Post Office is the visible form of the Federal Government to every community and to every citizen. Its hand is the only one that touches the local life, the social interests, and business concern of every neighborhood....The only method I can suggest by which all their desires may be gratified, is not merely to talk about the application of business principles to the Department; it is to apply them.
>
> It is not to work in poor quarters; it is not to transport mails on foot when they should go in railroad trains; it is not to tolerate disloyal or listless employees if better ones can be had; it is not, finally, to keep abreast of the times; it is always to lead the times. [1]

RURAL FREE DELIVERY OF MAIL

A MAJOR DEVELOPMENT WAS THE RESULT OF WANAMAKER'S RESOLVE to extend free mail delivery to every American family, particularly those who lived in the country. Believing that it was unfair to expect farmers to go into town to get mail, Wanamaker stated that it was the responsibility of the government to deliver mail to everyone without exception. He initially secured a small appropriation of just $10,000 for a limited test, but it was adequate to move the issue to the fore and to stimulate public demand for service that had been denied rural residents.

Opposition was widespread from those who predicted exorbitant costs and an enormous deficit for what they called an unnecessary and extravagant service. Moreover, said the opponents, roads were in such poor condition that mail delivery would be impossible in many areas. In true pioneer spirit, Wanamaker saw the building of better roads as one of the benefits of an improved mail system. He expressed his concern that if poor roads prevented mail delivery, then they also prevented children from getting to school and said, "Better roads mean a better America."

Rural free delivery, or what he called "country mail," became a reality across the nation in 1896, after Wanamaker had left office. But he had the satisfaction of knowing that he had proposed an idea that did not die.

THE PARCEL-POST SYSTEM

SIMILARLY, WITH PAINSTAKING EFFORT, he promoted the parcel-post system despite unified opposition from private express companies. They accused him of trying to advance sales in his own clothing business through low-cost delivery. Though he firmly believed in private enterprise, he felt the government should control and operate some public services lest private investors take advantage of the public and exact exorbitant fees for their services. Wanamaker did not trust large companies owned by stockholders whose primary concern seemed only to be the profits they could earn. It was a patriotic duty to provide a service that the public deserved. It was right, therefore it was possible.

Despite his efforts, there were too many obstacles to overcome, and he left office before Congress approved such a sweeping change. But his diligence was rewarded when on January 1, 1913, at 12:01 a.m. he was given the honor of sending the first parcel-post package mailed from Philadelphia.

John Wanamaker, at left, mails first parcel-post package from
Philadelphia, 12:01 a.m., January 1, 1913

COMBINING THE TELEPHONE, THE TELEGRAPH AND THE MAIL

CONTINUING HIS CRUSADE TO MAKE THE GOVERNMENT more people-oriented, he suggested that the fledgling, though promising, telephone industry and the telegraph lines be taken over by the government to prevent the establishment of monopolies. His plan was to combine all forms of public communication under the administration of the Post Office Department. Service could then be extended impartially to all people on a non-profit basis through existing facilities and current personnel. Competition would be eliminated and the public interest would be better served. Reporting to the President he wrote, "I want to see the two great servants of the people, the Post Office and the telegraph reunited, and the telephone brought in to enhance the combination." [2] He argued that the Post Office Department could supply telegraphy at less cost than could a corporation and that the public demanded cheaper telegraphy.

Facing financial disaster if Wanamaker's plan were adopted, and yet unwilling to publicly disclose their profits, the telegraph companies fiercely opposed his plan and fought to maintain their ownership. Not even a cooperative plan in which postal telegrams would be sent from local post offices through the telegraph companies was acceptable to them. It was a threat to their existence and was seen as an insidious attempt to undercut them. Despite his efforts, the postal telegraph never became a reality in the United States. But many years later, "deferred telegrams" or "night letters" did follow Wanamaker's plan and were commonly used throughout the nation.

BANNING MAIL LOTTERIES

IN OUR DAY WHEN STATE LOTTERIES are legal methods of raising money for worthy public causes, the moral issue of gambling is seldom raised. Government seems to have concluded that "good ends" justify whatever means are necessary to accomplish them. Moreover, the public seems willing to accept as "right," whatever has become "lawful." Wanamaker would not agree. He believed that lotteries, like other forms of gambling, were socially and economically harmful.

A national lottery had been initially authorized by the American Congress of 1776, but public opposition grew rapidly because many churches viewed legalized gambling as a moral blight upon the nation. A wide-spread debate ensued as preachers denounced lotteries for encouraging slothfulness and being detrimental to the values of faithful labor and frugality. Following the example of England's ending of lotteries in 1860, all American states except Louisiana outlawed lotteries by the time Wanamaker became Postmaster General in 1889.

The continued success of Louisiana's lottery was dependent, however, upon the United States mail as it attracted sales from out of state. With the encouragement of his many religious friends, Wanamaker successfully persuaded Congress to forbid the use of the mails for any lottery, even if an individual state gave its approval. Despite the appeals of the Louisiana state legislature, the Governor upheld the action of Congress until the Supreme Court concurred with Congress. This accomplishment brought great delight to the heart and soul of the Postmaster General.

THE POSTAL SAVINGS SYSTEM

AS ONE WHO HAD PERSONALLY LEARNED the value of saving money and using accumulated funds for sound investments, the Postmaster General envisioned enormous possibilities for a Postal Savings System. Wanamaker was aware of many foreign-born folks who chose to hoard their money in secret places at home because they mistrusted banks. He proposed that the U.S. Government offer a secure depository of funds with the same rate of interest offered by the banks. Deposits would be made at local post offices with the Government guaranteeing deposits and having the temporary use of the money as well. Circulation of the funds would help the economy of the nation while the individual depositor would be gaining interest at the same time.

But it was not until 1910 that Wanamaker's proposal finally gained Congressional approval and post offices began accepting deposits with 2% interest. The value of the savings plan through many years can hardly be estimated as deposits "peaked in 1947 at almost $3.4 billion, with more than 4 million depositors." [3] The system was terminated in 1963.

PNEUMATIC TUBES SPEED UP THE MAILS

WHILE ON A TRIP TO GERMANY, Wanamaker observed the use of pneumatic tubes for the rapid delivery of mail. (He had also used a similar system in his Philadelphia store to send money from numerous sales counters to the cashier's desk.) When he returned, he established the first United States pneumatic-tube mail line on March 1, 1893 connecting the Philadelphia Post Office with a nearby substation. The St. Louis Exposition of 1904 presented the first exhibit depicting pneumatic tube mail. In subsequent years, as the idea gained favor, more than 57,000 miles of tubes were put into operation in New York City, Boston, Chicago and St. Louis.

THE POSTAL MUSEUM

AS A VISIONARY OF THINGS TO BE DONE in new and surprising ways, Wanamaker, nevertheless, was also a student and preserver of history. It is a rare combination when one has the ability to be forward-looking and at the same time historically minded. Since the days of his youth, he had preserved his personal diaries, date and appointment books, as well as family and business correspondence. Whether he ever reviewed them is uncertain, though it is most unlikely, but he wanted them to be kept for the benefit of generations to come. How poor we would be without them today.

Similarly, he was committed to the idea of keeping the records of the Post Office Department intact.

> The earliest reference to a postal museum is found in the Post Office's Annual Report of the Postmaster General for the period ending June 30, 1887. One paragraph, alone, outlined the scope of what the collection should entail. Wanamaker brought the subject up again in 1889 shortly after he became the Postmaster General. While it was not his original idea, he was the one who was responsible for making it a reality. [4]

The United States Post Office Department, under his supervision, became a depository in 1890 not only of correspondence and other papers, but also of mail pouches, uniforms, insignias, photographs, maps and anything else that would document and illustrate the development of the Postal System. So many objects were submitted by postal employees, postmasters and even foreign countries that a room had to be set aside to accommodate them. The U.S. Congress appropriated $1,000 to cover the expenses and an additional $1,200 to employ a competent overseer. So impressive was the collection that $40,000 was added to the Post Office Appropriation bill to provide for an exhibit at the 1893 World's Fair in Chicago. All items were later returned to the Post Office Department for a permanent exhibit. By the time the museum officially opened in Washington on October 22, 1894, John Wanamaker's tenure had ended.

In 1913 Postmaster General Hitchcock decided that the Museum should not be the responsibility of the Postal Department and had the collection transferred to the Smithsonian Institution. Reactivated by a joint agreement between the U.S. Postal Service and the Smithsonian Institution in 1990, it has once again taken on its own identity. Financed and administered jointly by the two bureaus, The National Postal History and Philatelic Museum is part of the Smithsonian's Museum of American History. Located in the Old Post Office Building in Washington, D. C., it is "home for more than 16 million objects," all remaining in the ownership of the Smithsonian.

ONE OF THE MOST SIGNIFICANT DEVELOPMENTS in the United States Postal System during Wanamaker's tenure was the issuance of commemorative stamps. Having served as chairman of the Finance Committee of the U. S. Centennial in 1876, Wanamaker remembered the stamped envelope design that had been issued at that time to commemorate the one hundredth anniversary of American Independence and the excitement it created. It also became a revenue-bearing venture.

During the summer of 1892, The Post Office Department, under Wanamaker, determined:

> ...to issue, during the progress of the Columbian Exposition at Chicago, a special series of adhesive postage stamps of such a character as would help to signalize the four hundredth anniversary of the discovery of Columbus. [5]

Just a few months later, at the beginning of 1893, the first of sixteen stamps in the complete set was issued. Described as "the most glamourous of all United States issues," the colorful stamps depicted the story of Columbus "Soliciting Aid," "In Sight of Land," "Landing," "In Chains," "Presenting Natives," and in other settings. The first sheet of these historic and famous stamps went to the museum exhibit in Chicago and is today in the Smithsonian collection.

Though the stamps were an instant success, not everyone was pleased with them because of their new, unusual width and the cost ranging from one cent to five dollars. Many stamp collectors and dealers could not afford such an expensive investment. Nevertheless, the Department anticipated that considerable revenue would be secured through the sale of many stamps that would never be used for postage. Their report stated that "Stamps sold in this way will, of course, prove a clear gain to the Department." The same benefit exists in the present day as the Post Office Department continues to issue commemoratives at a steady pace with a large percentage of them being purchased by philatelic collectors.

The cultural and educational importance of commemorative stamps was also noted in his report:

> The collecting of stamps is deserving of encourage-
> ment, for it tends to the cultivation of artistic tasks and the

study of history and geography, especially on the part of the young. [6]

WANAMAKER'S FINAL REPORT

AS HE LEFT WASHINGTON AFTER LEADING THE DEPARTMENT for four years, Wanamaker looked back with a mixture of disappointment and satisfaction. He had felt quite limited by the refusal of Congress to act upon his recommendations and believed that the Post Office could become much more efficient and effective if the Postmaster General were given the power to act. On the other hand, he could only exult in the reality of knowing that he had raised the awareness of the public, the U.S. Congress

John Wanamaker, at left, entertains President Benjamin Harrison (center)
at Lindenhurst, 1889

I desire officially to recognize the important service you have rendered as

Postmaster

under the administration of President Harrison. Whatever has been accomplished in the advancement of the service has only been possible through the fidelity and zeal of those associated with the Postmaster General.

In making this acknowledgment of your valuable assistance I beg that in the future, whether in or out of office, you will continue your interest in the postal service and study to promote in every possible way its extension and improvement.

Your friend,

Jno Wanamaker

Postmaster General.

Washington, February 15th 1893.

One of 69,000 individually signed letters sent to local postmasters by John Wanamaker in 1893

The 2¢ stamp, shown above, was one of the Columbian Exposition Stamps issued in 1893 by John Wanamaker.

and more than 150,000 employees of the Post Office to the basic principles of a successful business: high ideals, fairness, diligence, cooperativeness, and the desire to find new ways of doing things better.

With a loyalty comparable to his employees in Philadelphia, a multitude of postal employees across the nation responded to the magnetism of Wanamaker's strong leadership, personal care and concern. Long after he had returned home, they maintained contact with him through letters and personal visits. He personally signed and sent a letter of appreciation to more than 69,000 postmasters when he left Washington.

His final report to President Harrison in December 1892 stated:

> If you intended that I should be content to fill up the days with signing vouchers, allowances, commissions, leases and the like, or to listen to applicants or their friends seeking places, you are surely disappointed....I have been ambitious to make the postal system of the United States as nearly perfect and as far-reaching in its usefulness as possible.
>
> The natural growth of the postal service in four years has been superb:
> - 5051 new mail routes established.
> - Number of P.O increased, 8,984 (offices now 67,567).
> - Steady improvement in service.
> - Establishment of Postal Museum.
> - Work begun on a new P.O. structure. Financial monetary savings of a million dollars in new contracts.
> - Sorting of mails on railway cars while in transit.
> - Bookkeeping system improved. New smaller stamps.
> - The new Columbian Stamp series.
> - Mail lotteries ceased.
> - Ocean post offices.
> - Country free delivery. [7]

Wanamaker continued to add to the list and to elaborate on his achievements as well as the problems he had encountered. He had entered the political arena as an amateur and experienced the brunt of the biases of cynics. As he left the shores of the Potomac, he did so with a stronger resolve to carry his crusade for reform, innovation and ethics in government to his home state of Pennsylvania.

The Political Years

THE FOUR YEARS THAT JOHN WANAMAKER SPENT IN WASHINGTON as Postmaster General from 1889 to 1893 were a great awakening for him. Politics elicited unexpected demands upon this unusually self-sufficient middle-aged idealist, demands that were distinctly different from his experiences as the head of a retail clothing business or as the inspirational leader of a Sunday School. Not that he was incapable or unequal to the task; rather, it was not what he anticipated. He had so many things he wanted to accomplish but was hindered from doing by having to deal with slow, stubborn and often obstinate politicians. In addition to this frustration, he was constantly accused of improper motives and hypocrisy by those who opposed his reforms.

But when he had completed his term of office, somewhat scarred, but certainly not defeated, he was ready for even greater challenges. Not viewing himself as a statesman, but knowing that the prestige he had acquired in Washington carried considerable weight and influence, he lent his support to those attempting to reform the Republican party in his home state of Pennsylvania. He entered the congressional campaign of 1894 as a speechmaker for the Republicans.

The financial panic of the preceding year had threatened all retail businesses. Wanamaker, even, had to borrow heavily on his life insurance policies to keep his business going. Drawing on this experience, in one speech he blamed the Democrats of the Cleveland administration for a tariff bill detrimental to the economic welfare of the nation and waved the banner of Republicanism, proclaiming:

> Soon there shall rise another Abraham Lincoln—not to
> free three millions of slaves, but to emancipate the land from
> the blighting curse of inadequate protection. [1]

Using his skill as a speaker and his ability to paint word pictures, he contended that Republicans would surely bring about the "sunshine of prosperity" so greatly needed and desired by all. When the election was over, the Republicans had scored enormous victories at both state and local levels by the help he had given.

Wanamaker discovered that he had personal political ambitions and found an enthusiastic response wherever he went. It is not surprising that he soon set his eyes upon a seat in the Senatorial election of 1896. In addition to his own money, it was certain he could secure adequate financial support from numerous businesses seeking representation for their common concerns.

Wanamaker failed in his bid for the senatorial seat. He tried unsuccessfully to conduct his own campaign without the aid of Matthew Quay, Pennsylvania Senator and Republican political boss, often called "King Matthew." Though Quay had enlisted Wanamaker's aid in helping to finance Harrison's presidential campaign in 1888, the two of them had been at odds for several years after Harrison chose Wanamaker instead of Quay for Postmaster General.

Quay made no pretense about his unmatched power and control gained at any cost and maintained by any means, ethical or otherwise. Wanamaker, on the other hand, opposed anything that even slightly appeared to be dishonest or unjust. After all, he had to face his Bible students each Sunday and attempt to live what he taught. Quay gave him plenty of reasons for concern.

MATTHEW QUAY—POLITICAL BOSS

OFTEN ACCUSED OF BRIBERY, intimidation, the misuse of state funds for personal gain and a disregard for basic social issues, Matthew Hanley Quay had indisputable control of a powerful machine answering his every whim. Called "the ablest politician this country ever produced," [2] he became one of the most controversial figures in American politics.

The son of a Presbyterian minister from the western Pennsylvania community of Beaver, Quay had at one time considered the ministry as a vocation but chose instead to enter politics. Quay joined the Republican party at its inception in Pennsylvania and used his superb organizational skills to dominate the political scene, often spilling over to the opposition party. In an age when personalities attracted more attention than issues,

Quay controlled the personalities. His enemies viewed him as a malevolent force incapable of doing anything justly or fairly. In their eyes he also appeared to be invincible.

After helping Andrew Curtin in his bid for governor in 1860, Quay was rewarded with an appointment to the Commissary Department of the State, but soon became the Governor's private secretary. He joined the Union Army in the Civil War and escaped injury and death in the brief but bloody battle at Fredericksburg. Colonel Quay was later awarded the Congressional Medal of Honor. Returning to Harrisburg during the last two years of the war, he was elected to the state legislature in 1864 for a one-year term in the House of Representatives.

Before long, Quay, the opportunist, saw the futility of supporting the bid of Andrew Curtin for U.S. Senator in 1867 and, surprisingly, joined the camp of Simon Cameron, later noted as the inventor of the modern Republican machine. Cameron, and his son J. Donald, dominated Pennsylvania politics until Matthew Quay elbowed his way to the top in 1879. By that time Quay had served as Secretary of the Commonwealth, a delegate to the Republican National Convention, Recorder of Philadelphia, and Chairman of the Republican State Convention.

Despite a brief respite when he returned to his home town of Beaver, by 1884 Quay had designed a new model of the political machine by reserving "political spoils" at the state level rather than the national level. No longer would it be an operation from the "top" down. Taking over as state boss, Quay controlled virtually all state appropriations to public institutions. When lawmakers realized he controlled funds for their own districts, they were forced to bow to his wishes, vote as he instructed them, and helplessly stand by as his empire of dominance mushroomed.

Quay was elected State Treasurer despite an earlier implication in a sweeping money scandal in the same department. He manipulated banks for political, if not personal, advantage and decided which banks would receive state funds on deposit and so received interest payments on the side. This gave him money to determine who would hold office and to manipulate elections as he pleased. He then made a successful move to the United States Senate.

Among the many critics of Quay's dominance of the Republican Party in Pennsylvania was John Wanamaker. Even before Wanamaker went to Washington in 1889, he had been urged by an independent group of distinguished leaders in Philadelphia to become the candidate for mayor. Now with the support of other business leaders appalled by corruption of city workers and demands for bribes, he became a spokesman for improved city services.

He targeted the despicable condition of the streets which created havoc with his delivery wagons and the cost of gas used throughout his store. Gas service was notoriously unreliable, because profiteering investors leased the city gas works. Protesting this, he maintained that any and all profits should be reserved for the city itself and used to lower the cost of gas for the consumer and to keep taxes down. His opposition against political corruption at every level of government brought him into favor with political reformers and other businessmen.

Unrest in the Republican ranks was widespread among businessmen in Philadelphia and Pittsburgh. Many were dissatisfied with James Donald Cameron, Pennsylvania's other Senator, now showing undesirable signs of his advancing years. He had advocated a policy of free silver, a heresy which caused many farmers to join businessmen in opposing his re-election in 1896. Even Quay expressed the idea that Cameron had become a political liability.

A CHAMPION OF CLEAN, HONEST GOVERNMENT

In the mind of some Republicans, John Wanamaker surfaced as the best candidate to succeed Cameron and to represent the great commercial and industrial interests of Pennsylvania.

When Wanamaker went to Washington to meet Quay, then Pennsylvania's Junior Senator but undisputed boss, he repeatedly attempted to make peace with his longtime adversary. But, adamantly opposed to buying his way into office, he returned to Philadelphia without Quay's support. He was more aware of the spreading corruption mandated by Quay and convinced of his own personal desire to engage in a public showdown with the Republican chieftain.

Quay, threatened by the loss of power to such a formidable opponent as Wanamaker, made a counter-proposal that Boies Penrose become the candidate of the "regular" Republicans, meaning those that he was able to control. A bitter fight ensued between Quay and those supporting the former Postmaster.

Wanamaker asked Edwin A. Van Valkenburg, a former Quay supporter and a respected Republican newspaper editor from Wellsboro, to be his campaign manager. He was ready for battle. His hopes for success were destroyed, however, when the Grand Jury indicted Van Valkenburg as a purchaser of votes. Guilty by association, Wanamaker was unable to muster the required number of votes in the state legislature and lost the nomination to Penrose, 133 to 76. The machine had won again. Interestingly, however, Van Valkenburg was acquitted of all charges after the election.

But all was not well nor peaceable in the Republican camp. The seventy-six members of the state legislature who had opposed Quay, met at the Philadelphia Bourse. They gathered together more than 400 leading Republicans and businessmen, representing fifty-five counties, to protest party misrule and legislative corruption rampant in the state under Quay. In anticipation of the 1898 gubernatorial election, they sought a candidate of high moral character, unquestionable integrity and a willingness to fight to rid the state of a political machine threatening the future of the business community.

GUBERNATORIAL CANDIDATE AND SPEECHMAKER

ALTHOUGH JOHN WANAMAKER WAS OUT OF TOWN, vacationing in Florida, he was their unanimous choice. At first he was reluctant to undertake such a responsibility, hoping that someone else would be willing to oppose the unrelenting corruption sweeping the party. He accepted the nomination because to demure would mean Pennsylvania's continued domination by Quay's machine. Ultimately throwing himself into the foray with unmeasured energy, determination, and a resolve to win, he said, "Somebody must begin. I am ready to do my part."

Promising to focus on issues and to keep the contest free from personal attack, Wanamaker said:

> I have no personal quarrel with Quay. I never speak of him as
> a person, but as the representative of the machine which he
> has made and holds the grip of a tyrant. [3]

How much more of a personal attack he could have made is not clear. Despite his disclaimer, it became obvious that he considered Quay and others in state offices to be dishonest, untruthful, corrupt, and dictatorial. He now had the chance to prove his accusations.

Though Wanamaker's reputation for truth, honesty, justice and reli-

gious fervor was widely known, it was his political speech-making across the state that soon caught people's attention. Not having sought the nomination and seeking only to fulfill a public mandate, he moved from cities to towns facing large and small crowds with a promise of political reform. It was a call to duty that he enjoyed immensely.

In the seventy-two days that preceded the convention, he criss-crossed the state delivering sixty-seven personally written speeches, each one distinctly different. Displaying his intellectual versatility, no two sentences in all those speeches were identical. He bristled, however, when it was suggested that someone else wrote his speeches, for he expressed his message in his own unique and convincing manner.

The Court Room in Lancaster was filled and overflowing when he gave his first speech on March 16, 1898 saying:

Corruption is at its worst and the commercialism of politics is the chief characteristic of Pennsylvania. I am here tonight to throw myself unreservedly and unqualifyingly upon the side of the people to regain their lost possessions in Pennsylvania. [4]

He described the legislative schemes of Quay affecting liquor licenses, state and county prisons, the Civil Service Commission, the Electric Light Commission, the School Book Commission, and the Capitol Building Commission as "corrupt and vicious." He called them:

...the daring conceptions of the political "Ringster"...upon which the layman looks with amazement and incredulity. [5]

With detailed statistics he accused Quay of misusing more than two-million dollars in interest that had been diverted from the state treasury to Quay's political machine. Money appropriated by the legislature for public schools had been withheld, and there was an attempt to further reduce the appropriations. "It was," he said, "a question between schools and saloons —books and breweries—and beer won." Wanamaker's adamant opposition to the liquor industry and his personal advocacy for temperance was obvious to all.

Excoriation of the machine was his primary purpose as he cleverly accused Quay of writing a new code of conduct with several commandments that began, "Thou shalt have no other gods but the Quay machine." So vicious were Wanamaker's attacks that after the election he was sued for libelous statements by the state treasurer but was exonerated by the court.

THE WANAMAKER PLATFORM

BUT WANAMAKER WAS NOT TOTALLY NEGATIVE. He hoped that people would understand his opposition to the corruption practiced by Quay. Spelling it out, he pledged radical changes in both practice and policy:

1. Every dollar of the State's money should earn at least 2 1/2 percent interest, and be paid into the State Treasury;
2. Payment of monies to the school districts when due;

3. Immediate return of personal-property tax monies to the counties;
4. Termination of payments to illegal machine items;
5. Investigation of the state printing contracts, often abused;
6. Examination of the State Treasury Department to unearth irregularities;
7. Shorten Legislature Sessions in order to save money;
8. Correct overcrowding and health problems in state charitable institutions;
9. Increase appropriations for public schools;
10. Assist private charities and educational institutions;
11. Build the long-awaited new State Capitol without further delay;
12. Reduce taxes;
13. Build better roads. [6]

Space does not warrant listing all his proposals. However, he had long been involved in the prohibition movement because of his religious convictions and strongly favored a tax on beer, stating that "buyers of beer become paupers—paupers become a burden on the state." Humorously enough, he won the support of the farmers as he opposed "with all my power any law to place oleo-margarine on any kind of footing with pure butter." Practical issues were extremely important to him in politics, just as they were in his business.

Refusing to be called a party wrecker, he proudly declared:

> I am a better Republican than the Chairman of the State Committee (Quay), who when asked if he would support me if nominated by the Convention, said that he did not know. [7]

Gallant to the end, Wanamaker fought valiantly to win the support of Democrats, but to no avail. Yet, so convincing were his arguments against Quay's machine that, when it became obvious that Wanamaker would not win, many of his supporters chose to vote Democratic rather than support Quay's hand-picked candidate William A. Stone, who ultimately won the Governor's seat. One writer noted:

Wanamaker waged a campaign against machine and legislative corruption that will go down in history as the most important political event of the closing decade of the century. [8]

The battle which Wanamaker had fought so vigorously was lost only temporarily. Opposition had grown so rapidly and strongly against Quay that when his term in the Senate ended the following year, the state legislature, consisting of a coalition of Republican and Democratic supporters of Wanamaker, refused to re-elect him. Relying upon the favor of Governor Stone, who owed his election to the machine, Quay was given an interim appointment, only to be rebuffed by the Senate which refused to seat him. His enemies finally scored a blow from which the Senator never recovered. Their rebellion had succeeded.

After the Gubernatorial campaign of 1898, Wanamaker returned to Philadelphia with enough political scars to justify a lesser political involvement from that point on. But as long as Quay or Penrose was in power, Wanamaker's efforts to smash the machine were not forgotten nor forgiven. Malicious gossip and scrutiny of his private and business life continued by politicians and political cartoonists. Though he was accused of failing to abide by customs and contract labor laws, no attempt to discredit or vilify his character ever succeeded. To the contrary, the integrity of Wanamaker, the prophet crying in the wilderness, was consistently upheld.

Now that he was past sixty, the appeal of political office diminished, but Wanamaker contributed more than $10,000 to the McKinley campaign and continued as a loyal Republican for the remainder of his life. When Theodore Roosevelt succeeded McKinley, Wanamaker tried to minimize the longstanding animosity directed against him by the former Civil Service Commissioner, now his President. The two strong-willed, independent-minded personalities, however, could find only their loyalty to the party as the basis for friendship.

Despite the views of his son Rodman and other close friends, Wanamaker chose Taft to succeed Roosevelt in 1908, believing that under Taft's administration business would start to swing upward after the panic of 1907. At his own expense, he placed a personally written document of support for Taft in every major newspaper across the nation and often spoke of Roosevelt as being unstable. He contributed a large sum of money to the campaign and when Vice President Sherman died during the campaign, there was a strong, but unsuccessful movement for Wanamaker to take his place.

AFTER THE ELECTION, TAFT AND WANAMAKER BECAME FRIENDS as the new President sought the advice of the experienced senior veteran of politics, devoid of personal ambitions. They met together in New York, Washington and Philadelphia, where Taft made a special visit on the last business day in 1911 just to dedicate Wanamaker's new, large twelve-story store, the first such act ever performed by a United States President.

During Taft's bid for re-election in 1912, Senator Penrose, Chairman of the Republican Committee, requested Wanamaker to attend the June Convention in Chicago in hopes that he would support the Pennsylvania machine. After a March meeting with Taft in the White House when he assured the President of his support, Wanamaker left for a vacation in Europe with the intent of returning in time for the Convention.

While he was away, and much to his dismay, the Progressive element of the party grew increasingly dissatisfied with Taft and hoped for a swing to Roosevelt who was more than anxious to return to Washington.

When Wanamaker's vacation, rest and health treatments in Europe came to an end, he embarked by ship for New York and hurried by chartered train to Chicago, arriving just as the initial balloting for Roosevelt and Taft was in process.

Three days later, when it appeared that the party would not be able to unite for either candidate, Wanamaker's name rose as a possible compromise candidate, but he quickly and firmly declined. Taft had already requested Wanamaker to second his nomination. Wanamaker acknowledged this as his patriotic duty in order to prevent what he considered an unnecessary change in administration. His loyalty to his friend was too strong to allow any weakening of support for his reelection.

Taft was finally nominated but in November was defeated by the Democratic candidate, Woodrow Wilson. Now seventy-five years of age, Wanamaker seemed content to put politics behind him and devote his remaining years to his two great stores in Philadelphia and New York as well as his continuing religious and philanthropic interests.

John Wanamaker: The Writer

It has been said that John Wanamaker could very well have been a writer if he had chosen to be rather than becoming a business man. Throughout his long career in marketing, he could not free himself from his fascination with the written word. His vocabulary expanded daily and he enjoyed expressing his thoughts and ideas with fresh terms as well as vivid and very picturesque phrases. He had no reluctance to coin new words like "*health-some-ness*" or, in describing the journeys of his wife, saying, "Mother *Pennsylvanied* all over." Writing to his son about business he said, "Such transactions after today are *unduplicatable*."

To emphasize a point he adapted the spelling to his own taste. "I *lub you*," he wrote to his son. Fascinated with creepy reptiles, he called them "*snaiks*" and described one as the "*rattlesnaik* whose skin is too short for him and don't quite cover all his bones and when he wiggles, they make a *nois*." Returning from one of his relaxing vacations he wrote to his sister, "I shall get down to doing something more *substanshuler* than living in *eyedulness* here!"

EVERYBODY'S JOURNAL

Before Wanamaker was thirty years old, he published *Everybody's Journal*, a monthly news journal of four pages "For Young Business Men and the General Public." Distributed without cost to customers in his store, it was also mailed to anyone providing an address and postage stamp. He copyrighted the paper and filed it with the Office of the Library of Congress in Washington. Documenting his endeavors was important to him and provided a legacy for those who followed him.

Originally begun at Oak Hall at Sixth and Market Streets, *Everybody's Journal* took on even greater significance when the new store was opened at Thirteenth and Market Streets. One issue, in addition to picturing the new building in line drawings, provided a very detailed description and accurate dimensions of the store.

> The shape of the building is a huge parallelogram, 250 by 373 feet in size covering an area of over 90,000 square feet or nearly 2 & 1/2 acres. There are five brick towers, 64 feet in height, each having its domes and minarets, and one surmounted by a large clock. The structure is but one story high, or 25 feet from ground to balcony, except in the wide central nave which is 48 feet high in the clear. There are forty huge bulk windows and ten wide doors for entrance and exit. [1]

Though much of the *Journal* was devoted to describing the goods and services the store provided, other articles were of general interest: biographies of city folk like Alexander Whildin, the leading wool merchant in Philadelphia; poetry and lithographic pictures. Practical philosophy, Wanamaker style, provided a balance to the promotional announcements. Advertising as we know it today was not included at first, but was added after Wanamaker purchased the New York store in 1896. The *Journal* then became an illustrated magazine, sold for 10¢ a copy and had a circulation of more than 100,000 by 1900. In 1911 Cyrus H.K. Curtis bought *Everybody's Journal* and changed the name to *Everybody's Magazine*.

THE FARM JOURNAL

IN MARCH 1877, *THE FARM JOURNAL*, VOL I, NO 1, was started in Philadelphia with Wilmer Atkinson listed on the masthead as publisher. John Wanamaker, however, claimed to be the originator, a claim that created a defensiveness on the part of Atkinson and his successors throughout the magazine's long and successful history. It is a dispute that will probably never be put to rest.

The Farm Journal provided practical information for farmers and their families and was devoted to the farm, orchard, garden and rural economy. It has enjoyed a favorable reputation for 116 years. The editorial policy first established by Atkinson excluded objectionable advertising and guaranteed the products it promoted. It gave assurance of financial restitution for any loses incurred by buyers, a policy much like Wanamaker's.

John Wanamaker opened his "new kind of store" at Thirteenth and Market on March 12, 1877, the same month that the *Farm Journal* began. He advertised in the *Journal* in an endeavor to reach rural families and to make up for the loss of tourist trade when the U. S. Centennial closed during the preceding year. His large full-page ads dominated the *Journal*, giving the impression that the new publication was the product of the fertile mind of this adventuresome and successful young man.

But nine months later, Atkinson, not wanting to be in Wanamaker's shadow, determined to show his independence and published the following disclaimer:

> The individual who continues to give currency to the story that *Farm Journal* is Wanamaker's paper is wanted at this office. We distinctly declare that not a person living has one dollar's worth of ownership in the *Farm Journal* except for the one whose name is at the head of this paper. [2]

Herbert Adams Gibbons, Wanamaker's biographer of 1926, reproduced a letter from Wanamaker of April 30, 1920 to Atkinson as follows:

> You will remember that I began the publication of the *Farm Journal* in the old Grand Depot in 1877. You were my editor until the little *Journal* had so grown that I felt the object I had in starting it was accomplished and turned the paper over to you without any price except your agreement to see that all its subscribers had my contract fully carried out for the subscriptions they had paid, which I think were twenty-five cents a year....
>
> ...It is a great pleasure I assure you, Mr. Atkinson, to extend felicitations and good wishes to you, my longtime friend, and to wish you, for the *Journal* which reflects your perseverance and personality, greater success in the years to come than it has ever enjoyed. [3]

One could surmise that simultaneously Atkinson and Wanamaker wanted to direct their attention to the farmers, one with editorial skills and the other with merchandise, and that they needed each other to accomplish their respective goals. Atkinson had been in the newspaper business for nine years and Wanamaker had goods to sell. Being assured of Wanamaker's continual advertising revenue would enable Atkinson to start the *Farm Journal*. At the same time Wanamaker could reach out to the rural customer through his advertisements in the magazine. It also seems likely that Atkinson would have been dependent upon Wanamaker's ready-made customer mailing list, which would account for the large initial printing. As stated in the first issue:

> There will be 25,000 copies of the first number of the *Farm Journal* printed and mailed to farmers and other rural residents, within a day's ride of Philadelphia. [4]

Wanamaker, a local store owner, would have reason to reach a limited geographical constituency. A publisher, on the other hand, would want as broad a geographical base as possible—even national—not just people "within a day's ride." Correspondence in the files also seems to indicate that Wanamaker may have provided direct funding for Atkinson which was later repaid after the *Journal* established a firm footing.

THE FARM JOURNAL

DEVOTED TO THE FARM, ORCHARD, GARDEN, AND RURAL ECONOMY.

A NATION'S GREATNESS DEPENDS ON THE VIRTUE AND INTELLIGENCE OF ITS FARMERS.

Vol. 1.   PHILADELPHIA, MARCH, 1877.   No. 1.

PUBLISHED MONTHLY AT

NO. 726 SANSOM STREET,

SATURDAY EVENING POST BUILDING,

At 25 Cents a Year.

WILMER ATKINSON,   - - -   *Publisher.*

Publisher to Reader.

THE FARM JOURNAL offers no terms to clubs, and no premiums to subscribers. The price of THE FARM JOURNAL is 25 cents a year.

There will be 25,000 copies of the first number of THE FARM JOURNAL printed and mailed to farmers and other rural residents, within a day's ride of Philadelphia. Subscriptions should be mailed direct to the Publisher, or they may be handed to Postmaster to forward. The Publisher will insert advertisements of an unobjectionable character, at 40 cents a line. No lottery swindles, cheap jewelry announcements, quack medical advertisements, nor Wall Street speculator's cards, can find admittance at any price.

The postage on THE FARM JOURNAL will be paid by the Publisher.

The Publisher does not intend to occupy much space with puffs of THE FARM JOURNAL, leaving it for the intelligence of the reader to discern merit, if any exist.

Enough said; send along the 25 cents.

Go West!

Yes, go to Kansas. If the grasshoppers do not overrun your farm, the prairie soil will yield a good crop; then you can send it to market and pocket the proceeds. You can get for butter—choice, 16 to 18 cents per pound; butter, medium, 12 to 14 cents; eggs, per dozen, 18 to 20 cents; corn, per bushel, 25 cents; oats, 17 to 20 cents; wheat, $1.05 to $1.25; rye, 50 cents; sweet potatoes, 50 cents; hay, per ton, $3.50 to $4.50; chickens, per dozen, $2 to 2.25; chickens, dressed, 4 to 5 cents per pound; turkeys, per pound, 8 to 8¾ cents per pound; cabbage, per head, 10 cents; cheese, per pound, 12 to 15 cents; wood, per cord, $4.50 to $5.

Go West, young man, go West !

Strawberries—Essex Beauty.

BY WILLIAM PARRY.

As the time approaches for setting out strawberries, it may be well to consider what kinds to plant. In the early stages of strawberry culture, when it was difficult to raise enough to supply the demand, the main question was What kind will yield the most bushels, and bear transportation best to market? quality not claiming much consideration, as any strawberry that looked well, was considered good enough to sell. Then the general sentiment was in favor of Wilson's Albany, which was very productive, turning red before it was ripe and palatable, could be carried a greater distance to market than other more delicious berries, which did not color up well until they were ripe enough to eat without sugar. Now we have many varieties, large and excellent, and if they are not so generally adapted to all soils and climates as the Wilson, some of them can be found to thrive well wherever the Wilson does, and are of much better quality; among which may be named: Charles Downing, Colonel Cheney, Captain Jack, Cumberland, Triumph, Great American, Jucunda, Kentucky, Monarch of the West, Seth Boyden, Triomphe d'Gand, and others—large, luscious, and sufficiently productive to supply the demand; and sometimes, when the markets are overstocked with berries, the Wilsons are left unsold for the want of purchasers.

The accompanying engraving is intended to represent a medium-sized berry of a new variety, recently introduced, called

ESSEX BEAUTY.

being four and a half inches in circumference. It might be called large, compared with the berries most commonly seen in market; yet we have measured berries of the same variety six and a half to seven inches in circumference. It was raised from seed by E. W. Durand, who also originated the Great American, and is second in size only to that wonderful strawberry, single specimens of which have measured nine inches in circumference and weighed from 2¾ to 2¾ ounces each. When exhibited at the U. S. Centennial Exhibition last summer, the International Judges of the Pomological Department were of the opinion that the flavor of the Essex Beauty was superior to that of the Great American. Ripening earlier than the Great American, and of superior flavor, it possesses in a high degree two good qualities, much sought after by producers and consumers. Both varieties are of a beautiful, bright, crimson color, excellent qualities, firm and very productive, yielding from thirty to one hundred berries to a single plant, and frequently more than a quart to a hill.

They are both desirable to cultivate, and should be grown in preference to the small, sour Wilsons, which have been grown in such quantities as to overstock our markets. A neighbor of ours last year sent to market in one day four wagon-loads of Wilson strawberries (120 crates), which sold at 12½ cents per quart. Another person sent to the same stall, on the same day, one load (30 crates) of large, sweet strawberries, which brought 50 cents per quart, yielding as much money as the four wagon-loads of Wilsons, with only one-fourth the expense for picking and hauling to market.

CINNAMINSON, N. J.

Sheep on the Farm.

BY EASTBURN REEDER.

In successful sheep husbandry at least three conditions are essential

First. Location and adaptation of the farm for the business.

Second. Adaptation of the breed to accomplish the object sought—mutton, wool, or both combined.

Third. Care and skill in their management.

There are very few farms but what are well adapted to keeping sheep. If the surface of the ground is not too wet, sheep will do well almost anywhere. There are many farms that will perhaps pay a better return for the investment if devoted to dairying or general agriculture. It is upon those farms which are unsuited to the purposes of grain raising or dairying that I would urge the claims of sheep husbandry. Steep hillsides, broken and new land, rocky and stony places, will often make excellent sheep pastures, and cannot profitably be devoted to anything else. There is much land of this kind which is now producing nothing but briars and weeds, which, if stocked with sheep, would contribute much to the owner's income. The value of sheep as aids to the farmer in subduing weeds and briars is not sufficiently understood or appreciated. But while it is true that sheep can be kept profitably upon land that cannot be well be devoted to anything else, it is still equally true that upon good land, with care and skill in their management, they will pay as well as any other kind of stock, and with less labor to secure it.

As the principal object sought to be produced, mutton or wool, so should the farmer be governed accordingly in selecting his stock of sheep. Where land is high, and hay and grain bring good prices, it will not pay to keep sheep for the purposes of wool-growing alone. On such land and in such locations the value of the carcase must be combined with that of the fleece to make the business remunerative. The average amount received for the wool of a single sheep ranges from one to two dollars at present prices. On land worth $100 an acre it will not pay to keep sheep for wool-growing when hay is $20 a ton, or corn 60 cents per bushel. The relative gross receipts per acre would stand in something like this proportion :

1 acre of land, cutting 2 tons of hay, worth $40.

1 acre of land, yielding 50 bushels of corn, worth $30.

1 acre of land, pasturing 10 sheep, yielding wool, worth $20.

But if these 10 ewes each produce a lamb worth four or five dollars, then the gross receipts per acre will be swelled above that received from either hay or corn. It is no uncommon thing for the farmer to purchase say 20 ewes for $5 apiece, making $100 for the lot, and before the expiration of a year to sell $25 worth of wool, and lambs amounting to $80 or $100, making over 100 per cent. on the investment, and have the original stock on hand, worth as much or more than at the time of starting. Of course this is not all to be set down as profit. Neither is the whole amount received for a crop of hay or grain to be considered as profit. In determining the actual profit on any crop there are many items of debit and credit to be counted before the true result is reached. In sheep husbandry the credits come in under the heads of wool, lambs, mutton, manure, improvement of the farm, etc., while the principal charges are for provender consumed and labor in their care.

Though Wanamaker persisted in his claim that he started the magazine, Atkinson never contradicted the claim—even in his autobiography. He simply disavowed any ownership or control by anyone other than himself. His careful use of words in his disclaimers leads this researcher to conclude that both men were right in what they said.

THE TIMES PRINTING HOUSE

As an avid reader and lover of books—though devoid of any formal education beyond three years in grammar school—John Wanamaker encouraged everyone he met to read. He had learned that one's own experiences are vital for a good life but not sufficient in themselves. It is through the experiences of others, as related in books, both fiction and non-fiction, that one's understanding of the past and vision of the future can be meaningfully enhanced.

Realizing that the average person had little opportunity for schooling, Wanamaker used his own financial resources to publish tracts, periodicals, booklets, and books and distribute them in his store and at Bethany Church. It was a project beginning in 1858 and not ending until his death in 1922. In 1874, prior to the opening of the Grand Depot, he established the Times Printing House just a block away from his store, Oak Hall. (It was typical of him to create, buy or build whatever was necessary to fulfill his public-spirited concerns.) His printing presses were run first by steam power and then by electrical motors. Many of the books and booklets he published, still found today, carry the imprint of the Times Printing House.

A sampling of Wanamaker's publications includes:
Guide to Philadelphia and the Wanamaker Store
The North American Indian, A Wanamaker Primer
"The Story of Nero's Emerald"
"Annals of the Wanamaker System"
Abraham Lincoln, A Wanamaker Primer
The Rule of Four, A Wanamaker Primer
"A Short History of the French Revolution"
A Friendly Guide Book to Philadelphia
The World's Greatest Organ
"Philadelphia Store News"
Acorns From the Great Oak Hall

ONE OF WANAMAKER'S MOST SIGNIFICANT PUBLISHING ENDEAVORS was the *Book News Monthly*, a magazine devoted to book reviews. First published in 1882 and containing 60 to 130 pages, it included "Bookish Matters of Interest," many illustrations from recently released books, a plate-paper portrait each month of a popular author and a descriptive price-list of over 3000 books. Initially the magazine cost 5 cents a copy or 50 cents for a year's subscription.

Once called "the foremost distinctly literary publication in America," it aided in making Wanamaker's Book Department the largest and most important retail book business in the United States by 1887. His store policy of "one price for everybody," carried over to books as well, and his price seemed always to be the lowest that could be found. At one point, book sales accounted for nearly a tenth of the total daily sales throughout the store.

Mother Wotsat (from The Wotsat Club, *a booklet for children) who will answer children's questions, "What's that?"*

THE SUNDAY SCHOOL TIMES

As Wanamaker prepared his weekly Sunday School lessons for the Bethany folk, he knew the value of Bible commentaries and other lesson helps, but not all teachers had ready access to such resources. The *Sunday School Times*, a weekly publication begun by the American Sunday School Union, attempted to fill the need but was on the brink of financial failure in 1871 when Wanamaker came to its rescue. Despite his other commitments, he bought the paper and managed it in the same businesslike manner as his stores. President Grant allowed him to print a letter of endorsement in one issue in 1876 which was distributed to all visitors of the U.S. Centennial in Fairmount Park and attracted thousands of new subscribers.

By 1877, the magazine had a rapidly expanding national circulation and the editing skill of Henry Clay Trumbull, one of the nation's foremost Sunday School leaders. Wanamaker relinquished ownership to Trumbull, his longtime friend who made the paper a "national institution among Protestant churches." Though not the originator of the *Times*, Wanamaker was responsible for its time-honored importance in providing an unprecedented educational and inspirational foundation for the Sunday School movement of America.

ANNIE E. MCDOWELL LIBRARY

A further indication of Wanamaker's fascination with books and his desire that others would always have access to great literature was the establishment of the Annie E. McDowell Library for the benefit of employees in the store. In a letter to this former employee and friend on June 23, 1887, he simply stated:

> I hear this is your birthday, and as I want to establish a library for the convenience of our womenfolk—many of whom I am sure must be great readers—I will make this the time to do it. With your permission it shall be known as the McDowell Free Library, in honor of a woman who has spent her life as a worker for women. I wish you would consider yourself with others herein named, a committee to select the best books, locate the cases, make the rules, and put the library into operation as quickly as possible. [5]

In 1904, he also provided a building and operating funds for the John Wanamaker Branch of the Philadelphia Free Library located on South Street between Twenty-first and Twenty-second Streets on land that he owned.

Reference must also be made to the prolific distribution of books by both Wanamaker and his wife to friends everywhere. Their personal correspondence includes many comments about books they had enjoyed and were sending as gifts. In addition, books like *Little Canary Stories*, *Sentimental Tommy*, *Black Beauty* and *Twice Told Tales* became Wanamaker's gift souvenir of each year's anniversary at Bethany. This writer possesses several books presented to one of his pupils, Jennie Love, in which one book-plate states:

> 1858-1899, observing forty-one years of the happy life of the Bethany Sunday School, Philadelphia, Thursday and Friday, February 16th and 17th. This anniversary reminder is with the Superintendent's regards.
>   John Wanamaker [6]

In *Out of the Deep of Suffering and Sorrow* by Charles Kingsley, John Wanamaker wrote, "To my dear friend Jennie Love, December 8, 1910," and signed it with his initials. It had been carefully selected by Wanamaker and sent following the death of Jennie's mother.

CHURCH HYMNALS

AS AN ACTIVE SUNDAY SCHOOL AND CHURCH LEADER, Wanamaker advocated a strong music program at each service. Congregational singing was as vital as the lessons taught from the Bible, for it was a unifying element and enabled worshipers to personally express their faith. Teachers offered instruction in a variety of musical instruments and the Sunday School orchestra provided the pupils an opportunity to demonstrate their newly acquired skills.

Many gospel hymns and songs were written specifically for Bethany Sunday School. Hymn writers and composers like William J. Kirkpatrick, Fanny Crosby, P.P. Bliss, John J. Hood and F.R. Havergal were friends of Wanamaker in the early days, with others, like B.D. and A.H. Ackley and Homer Rodeheaver, coming later.

The choirmaster at Bethany, John R. Sweeney, Mus. Doc., was a pro-lific composer of tunes such as "Tell Me the Story of Jesus" and "Take the World and Give Me Jesus," with words written by Fanny Crosby, and he also collaborated with Wanamaker in publishing *Living Hymns* in 1890. It was a compilation of hymns and "Orders of Worship for the Sabbath School." Wanamaker contended that in 1860 he had introduced the order of service that became a model for Sunday Schools throughout the nation.

Living Hymns was printed in various formats but always with the preface carrying signatures of recommendation by Wanamaker and two ministers of the church, Dr. J. Wilbur Chapman and Dr. J.R. Miller. Wanamaker also owned the copyrights of numerous songs and hymns dating from 1875 to 1898.

A few years before his death he encouraged Bentley D. Ackley, the well-known former song leader of evangelist Billy Sunday, to enter the hymn-publishing business. Wanamaker provided the necessary financing for him. The book *Hymns of Blessing for the Living Church* was published in 1916 with Wanamaker's commendation in the "Foretoken."

LADIES' JOURNAL

THE LADIES' JOURNAL WAS ANOTHER CREATION of John Wanamaker who had expanded his men's and boys' clothing store to include fashion merchandise for women. The third issue of the paper in September 1879 carried an excerpt from the Philadelphia *Times* which read:

> The second number of *The Ladies' Journal*, published by John Wanamaker and edited by Mrs. Mary F. Lambert is a great improvement on the first. It contains a number of special features which commend it to the popular reader—a bright little story by Ella Bassett Washington, of Virginia; poems by the editor and others; sketches of summer places in the mountains and by the sea, and a hundred attractions which will make it popular with ladies in all classes of society. The paper is printed for gratuitous circulation, and will be sent to any address forwarded to the Grand Depot, but it is superior, in most respects, to many papers, sold at a high price. It is well written, original, bright, and an undoubted authority on all things pertaining to the fashions. [7]

Because his store was a major importer of European fashions and merchandise, the advertising significance of *The Ladies' Journal* for Wanamaker at that time cannot be overestimated. It was exactly what he needed and hoped for as women became the primary clientele for his ever-expanding emporium. But it was not so much a change in focus as an expansion and enlargement of his desire to clothe the whole family and provide everything needed in the typical home. Obviously, Wanamaker's pioneer endeavor and success with a woman's magazine opened the way for others to follow.

Four years later in 1883, Cyrus H.K. Curtis, a young publisher of *The Tribune and Farmer*, decided to add a new section called "The Household" to his four-year-old weekly newspaper. When his wife read the articles he had clipped from other sources, she declared that she could do better. She started the next week as editor of the column, and her efforts increased the size of the feature as well as the number of subscribers. This led Curtis to abandon the publication, and in December of 1883 he created an entirely new publication using the same name—*The Ladies' Journal*—as Wanamaker's. Incomplete records make it seem likely that Wanamaker had ceased using the name and that another in-store publication called "Home and Store" had taken his *Journal's* place.

Because of a fireside scene labeled "Home" that was pictured on the cover of Curtis' *Ladies' Journal*, it was frequently referred to as *The Ladies' Home Journal*, a title it has retained to the present day. The remarkable story of the success of Curtis aided by his son-in-law Edward Bok is a phenomenon in the publishing industry equal to that of John Wanamaker in the mercantile world.

It is noted that Curtis and Wanamaker enjoyed a very favorable friendship through the years and kept up a lively correspondence as well.

Editorials of John Wanamaker

THE POPULAR WANAMAKER EDITORIALS in Philadelphia newspapers each day were personally written by John Wanamaker. They were his unique way to show that he was still in control of the stores even after he had relinquished much of the daily responsibilities to his son Rodman and other associates.

As part of store advertisements spread across a full page of the newspaper, his editorials, placed in a well-chosen corner, attracted as much attention as the merchandise that was for sale. People regularly purchased the paper to read what Wanamaker had written just as they would any other columnist.

Wanamaker began to write editorials in 1912 when he was seventy-four years old. The new, large, twelve-story building in Philadelphia had been completed and his son Rodman was capable of overseeing the business, as vast as it was. The Founder needed to undertake something new.

After the vigorous Republican Presidential campaign in Chicago, where Wanamaker had made the seconding speech for the nomination of William Howard Taft, he was back at home resting. Rodman, noting that his father was doing little more than reading and resting, suggested that he write some advertising.

Though at first reluctant, Wanamaker later gave in to the pleading of his son and began one more aspect of his fruitful career.

> I took up an old envelope, cut it open on three sides so that it unfolded completely and then started to write on the inside of it. It works very nicely. When I reached the bottom I found the envelope wasn't long enough, although an envelope ought to be long enough for what a man has to say. But I wanted to say more, so I took another envelope, and finally

a third one. I sent them to my son, supposing I had seen the last of them because there didn't seem to be anything special in them. The next morning I saw them published. [1]

At the end of ten years—between the ages of 74 and 84—he had written over 5,000 editorials with 4,000 of them appearing in his advertisements.

His subjects were always varied and interesting. No one could possibly predict what the next day's topic would be. Who could skip over titles like the following:

"That cow will never know what her tail is worth, until she loses it."

"My mother's kiss made me a painter."

"It is a pleasure to remember a day in Edinburgh."

"Sitting in a railway car in the station...."

"Some people are slow in cutting their wisdom teeth."

Wanamaker was a keen observer of nature and beauty. Inspired by a sunrise or sunset, the clouds or the blue sky, a robin or a squirrel, he seemed to derive a message of hope, optimism or courage from even the most ordinary sights and sounds which others often missed. He wrote, "Even a blind man by feeling can see the wondrous marvels of the sunrise at sea."

Patriotism was a favorite topic. During wartime he proclaimed: "The dress mostly admired today is made of khaki." He announced, "The Liberty Statue in New York Harbor is an inspiration even on a foggy morning before sunrise." Optimism was a keynote.

On national holidays, he recalled Lincoln, Washington, Stonewall Jackson, General Lee or General Grant. But never did he forget the ordinary person.

Philosophical, ethical and moral, his messages of good will often included practical business policies and up-to-date reports of the Wanamaker store.

As an advocate of education he told his employees and the general public, "Try to learn some one thing each day; it is the only way to get farther ahead in your chosen world."

In a review of hundreds of his editorials, one thing is quite apparent: Wanamaker, as devout as he was, never coerced his business associates or customers to accept his strong sectarian religious beliefs. Though unapologetic in his faith as a proclaimed follower of Christ and a believer in a Biblically centered theology, he nevertheless respected every person's faith as sacred. He wrote only of those virtues and values commonly accepted by all.

In the last year of his life he wrote a farewell editorial to his business associates, friends and to life. When the advertising manager received it, he apparently did not think it was appropriate for publication at that time and withheld it until the week following the Founder's death in 1922. It was read first to his employees in the store at a memorial service and then released to the public on December 19, 1922.

> **Some day not so far distant my little pencil** will have written its last piece and be laid aside.
>
> With simple, heartful gratitude to the many who have written me encouraging letters, and others who have personally sought me with thankful words, I write these heartful lines to say that what at first seemed a task became a pleasure, because I felt in my own soul almost everything I wrote, and desired, as I put it down in words, to be helpful to those fellow-pilgrims on the way with me.
>
> Much that I have said came out of my experience and observation; and much that I quoted was said by people that I had personally known in this country and across the sea. I refer to Henry Drummond, Professor Blackie, Charles H. Spurgeon, Newman Hall, Lord Shaftesbury, Martin Tupper, President Grant, President Garfield, President Harrison, President McKinley, James G. Blaine, President Taft, George H. Stuart, A.T. Stewart, Horace Greeley, D.L. Moody, Bishop Simpson, Albert Barnes, John Chambers, Judge George B. Orlady, Theodore Roosevelt, Anthony J. Drexel, Jay Cooke, John H. Converse, Henry Ward Beecher, John B. Gough, Sir George Williams, J. Russell Miller, George F. Pentecost, Horace B. Claflin, Marshall Field, John V. Farwell and others.

I have read and searched and listened to wise men and made the best use I could in the little scraps I have written of everything that I thought might be useful to others, struggling like myself to make the best of life.

The only wish I have is that I could have done all my work better.

John Wanamaker [2]

Our Best Friend Is the One Who Helps Us to Find Out Our Real

selves and who endeavors to show us how to make proper use of our abilities.

A school or college teacher who sees no other duty in her position than cramming heads with book knowledge alone is next door to a failure.

To help make the coming man somebody must study the headpiece and the heartpiece of every individual under his care and aid him to sift his book knowledge and apply to himself the part that will develop the plans of his life.

If he has no plans for his life, lose no time in helping him to find himself.

Let us be practical in keeping store and in everything else we have to do.

[Signed] *John Wanamaker*

Oct. 26, 1920.

One of more than 5,000 newspaper editorials written by John Wanamaker

Wanagrams

FOLLOWING THE TRADITION OF BENJAMIN FRANKLIN, another great Philadelphian he admired, John Wanamaker wrote epigrams and maxims and became the talk of the city.

Appearing first in his store publications to encourage his employees, they soon caught the attention of many others who grasped their broader meaning.

In the "Anniversary Herald" published by the store in 1908, the name "Wanagrams" first appeared. It is an apt title, for they reveal so much of the mind, disposition and character of the author himself.

MEN ARE GREAT ONLY AS THEY ARE KIND.

SHIRKERS GET PAID WHAT THEY ARE WORTH.

THE SWEETEST THING ON EARTH IS THE PLEASURE OF PLEASING.

REMEMBER THE WEEK-DAY, TO KEEP IT HOLY.

IF YOU WANT THINGS DONE, CALL ON A BUSY MAN. THE MAN OF LEISURE HAS NO TIME.

LET US NOT FOR AN INSTANT WALK BACKWARD.

LOVE IS NOT A COPPER WIRE. IT IS A SILVER THREAD. NO WIRE OR CABLE CAN BIND AS FIRM AND STRONG AS THE TINY THREAD OF LOVE.

A WORLD WITHOUT A SABBATH WOULD BE LIKE A

MAN WITHOUT A SMILE—LIKE A SUMMER WITHOUT FLOWERS—LIKE A HOME WITHOUT PICTURES.

HOW COMMON IT IS FOR IGNORANCE TO ADMIRE ITSELF.

NEVER DO TODAY WHAT YOU CAN DO AS WELL TOMORROW.

LIFE, LABOR AND LOVE—THE THREE WORDS THAT HOLD ALL THE NEEDS OF MEN.

CUSTOMERS HAVE NO SHORT MEMORIES.

SMILES ARE THE ROSES ALONG THE WAY.

A MAN MAY LOVE HIS BUSINESS, BUT HE NEEDS MORE LOVE THAN THAT.

CHRISTMAS IS A MAN-BORN; NOT A SENTIMENT.

NO ONE EVER SINKS WHO TRUSTS IN GOD.

HAPPY IS THE MAN WHO KNOWS HE WAS BORN TO WORK.

OBEDIENCE TO GOD'S WILL AND WORD IS NOT A HOLIDAY SUIT WORN ON SPECIAL OCCASIONS.

WHEN I REST, I RUST, SAYS THE KEY.

WEAR YOUR LITTLE PEARLS OF POLITENESS.

IT IS A PRIVILEGE TO HAVE A CHANCE TO HELP EVEN ONE PERSON EVERY DAY.

UNTRUTHFULNESS IS THE LEPROSY OF A BUSINESS LIFE.

The Letters of
John Wanamaker

THE PEN OF JOHN WANAMAKER WAS NEVER STILL. He could no more keep from writing than a bird could refrain from singing. With a pen or a pencil and a scrap of paper he expressed his thoughts as easily as water flows from a spring. He was at his best in the letters he wrote by hand. Though at times he was forced by the pressures of his business to dictate letters to his secretary, most of these were accompanied with an apology.

Often a single sentence seemed sufficient in replying to a customer or an invitation to deliver a public address. Time was always at a premium but courtesy and friendship were essential even toward people he did not know. When he had to state his case with firmness, it was always in a gentle manner. Whether he was at home, in his office, on a train, a ship, his vacation houseboat or sitting on the platform at a public event, his pen was always in motion describing the event, the surrounding scene, or simply expressing his own thoughts and feelings.

When writing to his family, Wanamaker frequently signed his letters with a variety of terms that described his feelings at that moment. He created his own words and spelled some others phonetically.

One of the best ways to understand his nature and attitudes toward life is to read some of the numerous letters that have been preserved for more than seven decades. The letters below are printed just as he wrote them with his coined words and phonetic spelling. It is of interest to note by the dates how old he was at the time. Neither age, wealth nor prestige kept him from being natural in his relationships.

* * * * * * * * *

May 24, 1898

Dear Sir,

I fear I did not thank you for your last most kind and encouraging letter. I wish to do so now.

Yours sincerely, John Wanamaker

* * * * * * * * * *

May 27, 1898

Replying to your letter of May 26th, much as I desire to help in every good work, I cannot with the numerous demands upon me at the present time make a favorable response to your appeal.

Very truly yours, John Wanamaker

* * * * * * * * * *

I am loaded with duties. Dictated last night 130 replies that had accumulated.

* * * * * * * * * *

Thanking you for your note, I think I cannot wheel two wheelbarrows at the same time.

* * * * * * * * * *

In reply to your letter of April 30th, my hands are so full that I regret I cannot loan you the money you want. You had better obtain it from your friends in the neighborhood where you live who should be willing to help you make an honest living.

Yours very truly, John Wanamaker

* * * * * * * * * *

In reply to your letter of May 23, it will be very much better for you to earn the money to buy a bicycle. Be industrious and the bicycle as well as other things will come to you in due time.

Yours truly, John Wanamaker

* * * * * * * * *

Miss Elizabeth Pasterfield Gates:

Dear Madam,

Thanking you for your esteemed letter of the 13th of May, I beg to say that I go to sleep within five minutes from the moment I touch my pillow, so you see I do not need the treatment you so kindly recommend. I thank you for your courtesy.

With great respect, John Wanamaker

* * * * * * * * *

August 23, 1918
Bedford Springs Hotel
Bedford Springs, Pa.

Mrs. Elizabeth Fales:

Sister of mine so dear. I greet you with this kiss and embrace of love from the far off mountings of Western Pennsylvania. I am still a heavy drinker of the dope of the maggykneesyure spring that skips out of its rocky hiding place and comes softly to old people with a refreshing smile.

But I shall have to turn my strong back on Maggy of the rocks one of the first days of next week and toddle home. My, oh my, won't I be glad to see your dimple and your lovely smiles for which I came miles to enjoy your cunning wiles of which you have piles, naturally. You blessed Lizerbet, I loves you,

Sertun and shure, Jonathan

* * * * * * * * *

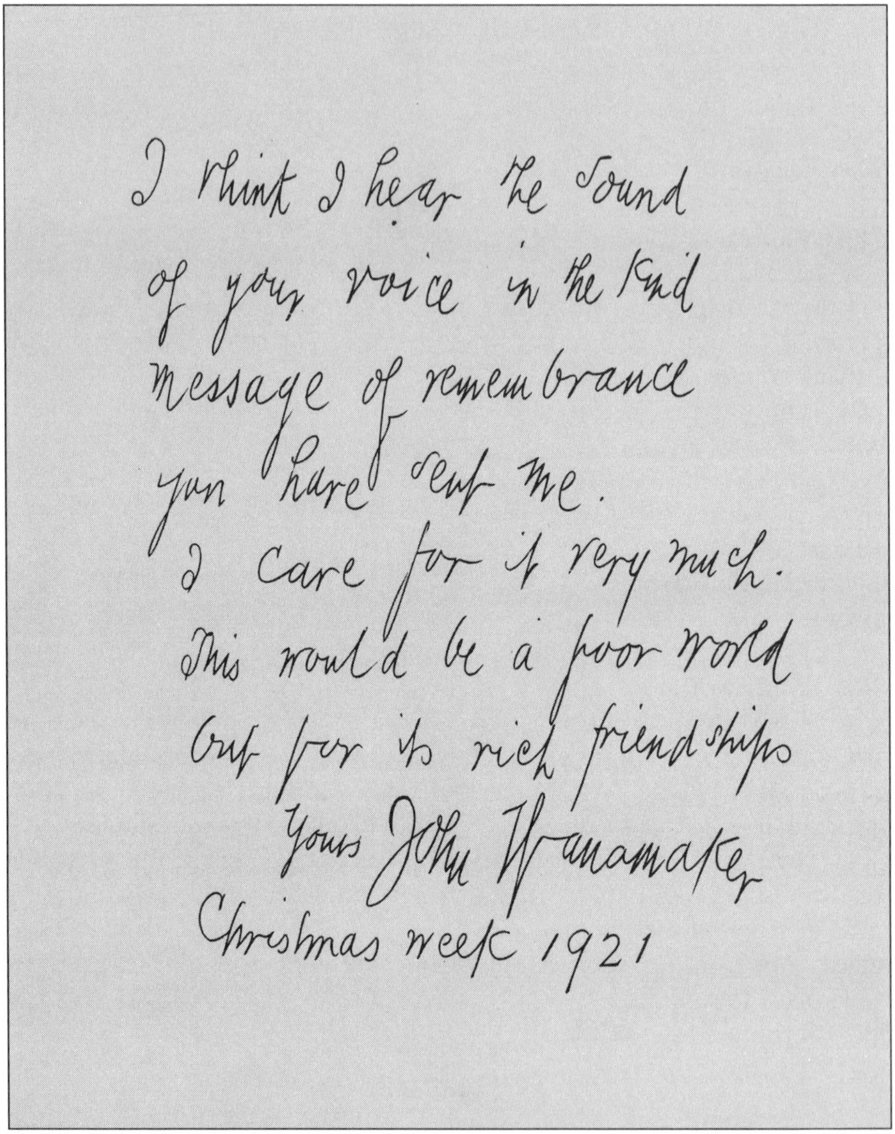

I think I hear the sound
of your voice in the kind
message of remembrance
you have sent me.
I care for it very much.
This would be a poor world
but for its rich friendships
Yours John Wanamaker
Christmas week 1921

July 1907
Germany - to his wife

Mother Dearest,
A rainy night and morning but clearing at one as I write. My cure goes straight on and I feel well....I never saw a more uninteresting crowd together than this morning....Such a gurgling, gargling, coughing, sneezing, wheezing, nose-blowing and throat-scraping and clearing lot I never did see or hear of before. With much and much more love to you and the kinder.
Father

****

16 Feb. 1916
Wednesday 9 o'clock
On board Nirvana
Out at sea
25 miles from Miami

My Precious Sister,
First of all my ship-load of love to you. This morning touch of you is much more from my heart than from my pen and as my hands are engaged in this morning greeting to you—why ? shouldn't I - put - my big - long arms - around YOU and squeeze YOU up a bit. I just tell you I feel like it....So I shall loiter about in this far end of the U.S. and fly home shortly to surprise you and do my own squeezing of you. With all the old time love and more.
Your Whenurabel Bruver hoping you and yurs is WEL.

****

May 17, 1905
Karlsbad (to his son)

My Dear and Precious Rodman,
Your letters are my jewelry these days. I am generous enough to wish that every man had a son as thoughtful of and good to his father....
With love firm and full, Thy Father

To his son Rodman

...I think the past year I have been drawn closer and closer to you as you fought so bravely through the difficulties that beset you. My love for you and your love for me makes life worth living and lightens all the tasks that fall upon us. I pray that we may be both spared to go hand in hand and heart to heart to do great things together for ourselves and all who are about us.

Yours with my whole heart - Father

* * * * * * * * * *

To his wife

Friday in the morn
March 8, 1918
on board Hibiscus
before breakfast
St. Petersburg

Most adorable-est Mary,

I am as well as little frisky Rodman, our occasional Lindenhurst boarder....We came over here at 11 a.m. yesterday....I attended the closing service and today I am taking the Evangelist Minister and his wife and the Resident Minister and his wife over to Passa Grille on the boat and having lunch with them on the boat....They are very nice people. I wish our house were open offener for such men with some of Moody's spirit in them.

* * * * * * * * *

7/22/18
To Rodman

Do be keerful of yerself this hot spell—we are neither stone or bronze and the bones of us IS very brittle.

* * * * * * * * *

Good night to you, dear Mr. Perfection, and all the love that your heart, shoulders and pockets can carry.

Your Old Johnathan Potterer

****

The Lord's own day, The first Sabbath in August 1918—and a gorgeous day it is....I clambered over the mountain before breakfast this morning and will never be able to tell of the odor of pine and other trees and the fresh beams of the new Sun on the Sabbath morning early decorating the forest with golden pillars as if it were the gateway to the Celestial City....

Always the same old lovingest Father

****

To his wife

My Mary, never so dear, good morning
On board Hibiscus 2/18/18
at 1/4 after 7

I rose to see the sun rise at 6:10 and got up and the sun is brighter than the newest piece of gold just out of the U.S.Mint. Dear good faithful Sun that smiles beauty and perfume in the flowers and life to everything that grows....

Ever and Forever

****

7 p.m., Friday, Feb.9 1905

My Precious Rodman,

My heart has a double throat in it as I write this to give you my birthday kisses and my best wishes for future days and years.

****

Letter To A Grandson

THE LETTER BELOW WAS WRITTEN BY JOHN WANAMAKER to his grandson John on his twenty-first birthday in 1911. It was originally written on small scraps of paper 3 1/2" by 4"—still to be found in his files—then put in final form. The hand-written letter actually sent was also recently found among the personal files of the grandson.

July 26th, 1911

Dear John:

I can hardly realize that on August first you will be twenty-one years old, and are entering upon the years of manhood. In another envelope, which I hand you with this, I give you in a well invested form a small present to mark the beginning of a new career in your life.

Bearing my own name as you do, I cannot but feel the most profound interest in every step you take. What you henceforth think, say or do, will make or mar the pride and happiness of your father, your grandmother and myself, and your many friends. Therefore, I am constrained by my love for you, to write to you out of the heart of an old experienced man a few of my thoughts that may be of value to you.

Life is a track much like a Railroad track. It is a single, straight track, and if you can back the train at all it is always at the loss of something.

Each of us are draughtsmen appointed to lay out our own roads with power to arrange them from the beginning clean through to the last mile. Each of us can fix our own levels and regulate all the grades. Each of us may determine and locate the stations along the route, stopping exactly where we like.

The stations that often almost settle themselves with many young men are Indolence, Impotence, Idleness, Inefficiency, Folly, Extravagance, Asthenia, Flash-in-the-pan, and Collapse.

But far better are such as I believe you will choose: Diligence, Integrity, Competency, Honour, Wealth, Happiness and Usefulness.

Each one's train is equipped to run wild of itself and when it does, it generally ruins all of the machinery and not infrequently it kills or cripples those who are nearest and dearest to us.

Every fellow at twenty-one automatically becomes the Engineer of a special train for life. He may climb up into the Driver's Cab and sleep until rust destroys the motive power. He can, if he chooses, play with his forces as if they were toys, and thereby impair their uses.

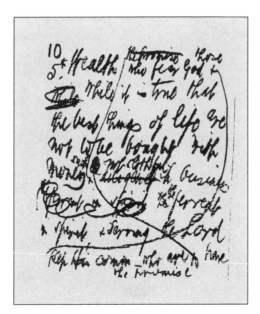

Facsimile of initial draft of John Wanamaker's letter to his grandson on his twenty-first birthday

He can by ignorance or carelessness upset his train into one of forty ditches to the sorrow of all his friends.

He can start and run well for a mile or two and then vacillate and zig zag until his friends give him up as not to be depended on for anything. But he can, if he will, master his forces, concentrate them and command them to do his bidding along the plain, straight road and reach safely and surely all the six stations, last named, for the blueprint map of a successful life.

The 1st Station—Diligence, requires only a resolute purpose and a conscientious daily effort.

The 2nd Station—Integrity, is gained by truth in word and deed, love and practice of honesty, and hatred and avoidance of deception and dishonesty.

The 3rd Station—Competency, is easily won by not spending money not in hand, paying promptly all obligations, not becoming surety for another, and by not lending or borrowing.

The 4th Station—Honour. The way to get there is a smooth track all the way. By true manliness in little as well as large things. Not making evil or keeping degrading associations, going face forward with cheerfulness and unflinching determination to every duty whether it be easy or hard to do. By not using intoxicating liquors and by never partaking in games of chance for money. By reverencing womanhood to the uttermost and living a clean upright life in thought, word and deed, making no compromise under persuasions or in self-evasions.

The 5th Station—Wealth. This is reached naturally after passing the previous stations. The best things of life are not to be bought with money. The fear of the Lord is the beginning of wisdom and in the keeping of His commandments there is the promise of great reward: "They that honor me, I will honor," is written in the Word of God.

The 6th Station is Happiness and Usefulness. This is the sure stopping place for such as make the maintenance of Character and Probity, the first essential in all their conduct.

So shall you win Capital Confidence and the approval and peace of your own heart, and the affection of your friends and fair people everywhere by a steady, undeviating, continuance along the path that your father walks to be your example.

Dear, dear John, I shall be near to you always to further in every way I can your life in prosperity, happiness and usefulness.

Yours faithfully, John Wanamaker

****

This grandson was the son of Louis Rodman Wanamaker who succeeded the Founder as the head of the Wanamaker stores from 1922 to 1928. The grandson, commonly known as Captain John because of his military service in World War I, later entered the business and worked until his death in 1934.

Letter to a Friend in Sorrow

John Wanamaker, 72 years old and a multi-millionaire, wrote by hand the following letter to a teen-age girl in his Sunday School at the time of her mother's death. The letter, preserved since 1910, was recently given to the author of this book by the family.

Wednesday, 1:30
November 30, 1910

Dear Dear Jennie,

I am crying with you in this greatest sorrow of your life because I know how sweet your mother was and because I love you and suffer with you.

It was only a few moments ago that the word came that your precious mother was at rest.

I stop all I have to do to come to you instantly with this letter of love and dearest, truest, heartfelt sympathy.

No word can tell you the feeling of sorrow I have for you and you can never understand how deeply I share in your loss because you do not know how deep and strong my affection for you is. I know your sensitive nature and how you cling to those you love and those who love you.

In such a time when the dearest of all leaves us to pass on to the Heavenly country, all we can do is to draw nearer to each other and rest the hearts that bleed upon those who love us, and help each other to lean upon the bosom of God, who never afflicts willingly and never mistakes.

Heaven and those already there, known and loved by

your mother, must be happier for her than even her old home on earth which you made so sweet for her.

We cannot see far with mortal eyes but we will trust the good God for what we cannot see or fully understand.

I will come to you whenever you want me. I love you and pray for you, dear, dear Jennie.

Yours ever, John Wanamaker [1]

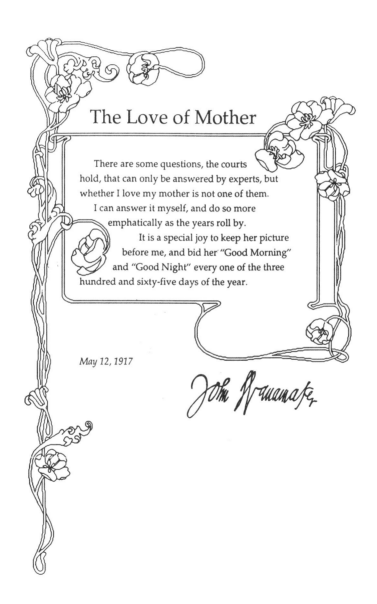

The Love of Mother

There are some questions, the courts hold, that can only be answered by experts, but whether I love my mother is not one of them. I can answer it myself, and do so more emphatically as the years roll by.

It is a special joy to keep her picture before me, and bid her "Good Morning" and "Good Night" every one of the three hundred and sixty-five days of the year.

May 12, 1917

Military Service Denied

JOHN WANAMAKER ALWAYS REGRETTED that ill health prevented him from serving in the Civil War. Nevertheless, in true patriotic spirit he recruited boys from his Sunday School at Bethany to enlist and support President Abraham Lincoln.

He and his young wife Mary were volunteers assisting Union soldiers as they passed through Philadelphia on the way to battle. He was also elected Secretary of the Christian Commission which was sponsored by the national organization of the Y.M.C.A. and provided welfare services among the wounded as well as those still on the battlefield.

The Draft-Exemption Certificate, seen below and indicating his tendency toward tuberculosis, was issued to Wanamaker in 1863 and was recently found among his papers at the Historical Society of Pennsylvania.

CERTIFICATE OF EXEMPTION FOR A DRAFTED PERSON ON ACCOUNT OF DISABILITY.

This is to certify, That *Jno. Wannamaker* of *Philad* _____ county, State of *Penna*, having been drafted, and claiming exemption on account of disability, has been carefully examined, and is found to be unfit for military duty by reason of *Phthisis* _____, and, in consequence thereof, he is exempt from service under the present draft.

Provost Marshal, and President of Board of Enrollment.

Member of Board of Enrollment.

Surgeon of Board of Enrollment.

DATED at *Philad*, this *26* day of *Sep* 186*3*

The Wife and Family of John Wanamaker

27

"The Great Wife of a Great Man"

SOMEONE HAS SAID, "Behind every great man there is an astonished wife." Not "astonished," but "astonishing" is the word to describe Mary Erringer Brown who became the wife of John Wanamaker in 1860.

Born in 1839, Mary Brown was the daughter of a Scotch-Irish grocer in Philadelphia. She developed a friendship with Mary Wanamaker, the younger sister of John Wanamaker, and they maintained a close-knit relationship throughout their lives.

Mary Brown and John Wanamaker got to know each other as young people when both were deeply involved in youth activities at John Chamber's First Independent Church. They shared a common faith and enthusiasm for religious meetings and community service. Mary, still in her teens, watched closely as John, the young Y.M.C.A. secretary, with boundless energy, spiritual commitment and lofty goals, developed a dynamic city-wide para-church organization. In her eyes, he was a man to be greatly admired and respected.

Mary, John, and Mary, his sister, started the Bethany Mission. They created a trio that did not scare easily, although on the first Sunday the South Street Rowdies chased them away. Returning the next week they planted the tiny seed that sprang up into a great church.

John's other sister, Elizabeth, soon joined them and stood by her brother in Christian service until the day of her death. Surrounded and encouraged by these three devout women all his life and with the memory of his loving and caring mother, John Wanamaker developed and maintained a kindly and caring disposition toward others not normally expected of a man in business.

For more than two years, while employed as secretary in the Y.M.C.A., John Wanamaker courted Mary Ann Brown, recording in his diary his frequent visits with her with a simple notation: "spent the evening with M___ ." [1]

While they were courting, Mary patiently waited in anticipation for those few minutes at the end of the day when he would stop by her home after work. She listened as he shared with her the experiences of his day in the Y.M.C.A. work or of his visits to a member of the Bethany Mission. He also told her some of the things he felt important enough to record in his diary:

> Heard Rev. McGuiness preach the best sermon in the morning I think I ever listened to. His text was, "They that wait upon the Lord shall renew their strength." O that it may never be forgotten. [2]

> Waldon W. died at 4 o'clock. Went to sleep in Jesus. I hastened to comfort them all. Oh, what would we do without the gospel in such hours? [3]

> Visited a dying girl—beautiful in death—so beautiful. [4]

CHOOSING A VOCATION

DID MARY EXPECT HIM TO BECOME A MINISTER? Would anyone be surprised if he did? Was he not at his best when he led the Sunday School? Did he know what the future held for him when he said:

> I feel as if God sent me to do a special work here. Have been providentially thrown in with two men—concerned about their souls. May the Lord bless the word so feebly spoken .[5]

Would Mary be content if he chose a vocation other than the ministry? Suppose that he were to embark upon a life of business—or even open a clothing store. After all, he did enjoy his years as a salesman with Colonel Bennett at Tower Hall. Would he have left it had he not become ill with tuberculosis and been advised by the doctor to go West?

Then too, there was Nathan, Mary's brother, who had learned a lot while working with their father in the grocery business. He and John got along so well together—maybe they could combine their talents and resources and open their own business.

One can picture John and Mary, sitting on the porch swing on a warm summer evening discussing the alternatives: the ministry or business. Must it be one or the other? Since he enjoyed both so much, could it be that somehow, in some way, he could muster enough energy to do both simultaneously? This was not a decision that he would make alone. Mary's opinion was of utmost importance to him, now and for the rest of their lives together.

After attending a Y.M.C.A. convention in New Orleans in 1860, twenty-two-year old John returned to Philadelphia having decided to leave the employ of the Y.M.C.A. and join Nathan in starting a clothing business while continuing the work at Bethany. His "lonely experience" in the South also gave him the determination to marry his sweetheart Mary. It was a decision that helped to make him a success throughout his life.

WEDDING BELLS

ON SEPTEMBER 27, 1860, Mary Ann Brown and John Wanamaker were united in marriage by their friend, Rev. Dr. John Chambers, the famous Philadelphia clergyman, at his large, 1500-seat church on South Broad Street. [Wanamaker said it was in this church "I gave my heart to God."] Curiously, the clergyman's Registry of Marriage book includes Mary's middle name Ann, not found in any other place. John's middle name, never used, is hinted at in the Landreth Sunday School visitation book of 1847 listing the four children of Nelson Wanamaker as "John N., 10 1/2; William, 8; Elizabeth, 5 1/2; Mary, 4." Most likely John carried his father's name, Nelson.

Mary and John, with little more than their love and their faith, began their venture of marriage residing at 2105 Walter Street [now Delancey Place] in a home they rented for $25 a month. John, at the same time, made notations in his diary of a beginning inventory for his new store:

> 6 business coats —cost $2.55—to sell at $3.50
> 6 spring overcoats—cost $6.82—to sell at $8.00
> 12 black alpaca —cost $1.46—to sell at $2.00

6 black alpaca—cost $2.91—to sell at $4.00
12 Marseilles vest—cost $1.28—to sell at $1.75
6 pants —cost $4.37—to sell at $6.00
24 pants —cost $2.55—to sell at $3.50

As Mary set up housekeeping in the rapidly growing city, her husband and brother opened Oak Hall, a men's and boys' clothing store at Sixth and High Streets, the center of the business area in Philadelphia. Knowing that [in those days] a woman's place was in her home and not in business, Mary determined that her husband would be free, from all domestic cares, a practice that she maintained for sixty years. At first, there was little money for home. Most of what John had saved from his salary at the Y.M.C.A. was committed to the store, and with the first day's sales amounting to only $24.67, the future did not seem optimistic.

Mary, with inherited frugality and an appreciation for even the most modest of accommodations and possessions, accepted the sacrifices made necessary by all pioneers. And pioneers they were in both their church work and their store.

Mary Wanamaker, wife of John Wanamaker

DURING THE FIRST YEAR OF THEIR MARRIAGE, Mary gave birth to a son, Thomas Brown Wanamaker, the first of six children—three sons and three daughters. Named after Mary's father, Thomas later entered business like his father and grandfather. But first, he and the children who followed had to have a quality education. Not having had the advantage of any formal education themselves, his parents were determined that no such deprivation would befall their children.

In 1879 Thomas entered Princeton University at a time when there were fewer than 500 students in the entire school. Obviously, higher education in those days was available primarily to the wealthy.

When Thomas graduated in 1883, his father gave him considerable responsibility at the Grand Depot located at Thirteenth and Market Streets. The business had continued to grow and now had over 2000 employees. Thomas took particular interest in the expansion of the physical property, making certain that facilities kept pace with the increase in sales. By 1885, his father made him a partner in business along with Robert C. Ogden, who had been persuaded to leave New York and join John Wanamaker, the nation's largest clothing store, in Philadelphia.

After marrying Mary Lowber Welsh at Holy Trinity Church in 1887, Thomas soon bore the enormous weight of running the business with Robert C. Ogden when John Wanamaker was appointed Postmaster General in 1889 and moved to Washington. Thomas was given "power of attorney" and was instructed "to take control and have supervision of all matters of business."

While John Wanamaker was awaiting Senate confirmation, Mrs. Wanamaker, her two daughters, Minnie and Lillie, and her son Louis Rodman were all in Europe for the year. When Thomas heard of the Senate's favorable vote, he wrote to her:

> My Darling Mother, I greet you as Postmistress General. All is over....Father is going to Washington tomorrow morning for the first time to begin his duties and I will go with him to see that he don't [sic] get stolen, unless I reconsider tonight. I think that perhaps I had better stay and look after the trade. I think that if you were here that is the advice you would give me.
>
> Write me, dear old girl, whenever you can. For I am

constantly thinking of you and planning for you. Goodnight now. How I wish I were on your knee and having my kiss from you.

Your Boy, Tom [6]

It is noticeable that the son was just as dependent upon the mother's advice as was his father. The love between them is revealed in his final comment about receiving her goodnight kiss.

Thomas was a brilliant no-nonsense businessman who disappointingly lacked the warmth and grace of his father. Seemingly concerned only with profits and often critical of employee inefficiency, he repeatedly expressed his concerns to his father with definitive impatience. At one point he stated openly that Robert Ogden, his father's business partner and long-time friend, had "outstayed his usefulness to the store." It was Ogden who, for the four years John Wanamaker worked in Washington as Postmaster General, had helped young Thomas keep the store on an even keel as it sailed forward. John Wanamaker would never have forgotten

Thomas B. Wanamaker, son of John Wanamaker

such commitment; a friend and colleague was a lifelong relationship, not an expediency.

Thomas controlled finances, expenses, profits and stock budgets. Each day he reviewed the sales sheets and stocksheets with the purchases and direct expenses of each department. If requisitions for supplies seemed too large, he would tear them up. Speaking favorably of him, a long-time employee of the firm said:

> Thomas was a check on the too ambitious plans of his father and the artistic expenditures of his brother Rodman. [7]

THE NORTH AMERICAN

SHARING WITH HIS FATHER SIMILAR CONCERNS for political reform, Thomas bought *The North American*, the nation's oldest daily newspaper, and used his editorial pen and publisher's power to strike out against all forms of political corruption. He attempted to stamp out the rampant vice which swept Philadelphia during the last decade of the nineteenth century. Civic regeneration and the restoration of ethics were frequent subjects of the editorial pages of his newspaper. *The North American* was often referred to as "John Wanamaker's Paper," promoting his ideas and puritanical views.

Showing his independence from his father and a bit of arrogance as well, Thomas announced plans for an up-coming issue of a Sunday paper, much to the dismay and sorrow of his father who considered it a desecration of the Sabbath. Taking five columns on the front page of *The North American* on Saturday, September 2, 1901, Thomas explained the Sunday issue to his reader:

> I, being the sole owner of the stock of *The North American*, including the real estate, I therefore control its policy and am alone responsible for its management....My father, Mr. John Wanamaker...has no authority whatever....His disapproval of and opposition to the publication of Sunday newspapers generally and particularly one owned by his son...constitutes a difference of moral opinion between us which I profoundly regret.[8]

Totally embarrassed by this move and unable to change his son's mind, John Wanamaker offered to buy the paper and keep it closed on Sunday. When his son refused the offer, John then approached the Session of Bethany Church and offered to resign as an elder believing that "any man who failed to rightly govern his family, did not qualify for such a worthy office." They rejected his overture.

For many years the elder Wanamaker had taught his Sunday School students that Sunday was a day of worship. Holding to his beliefs and teaching, he refused to conduct any business on Sunday apart from church work. When the United States Sesqui-Centennial was in the planning stages, Wanamaker, a strong promoter of the celebration, was nevertheless unwilling even to meet on a Sunday with Herbert Hoover, then Secretary of Commerce, who was in Philadelphia at the time to discuss the festivities.

To fully explain his position that "Sunday is the Lord's Day; it belongs to Him," John Wanamaker purchased space on the front page of *The North American* to respectfully differ with his son and publicly declare his opposition to a Sunday edition or anything else that would "destroy the Sabbath." To him, it must be "kept holy."

Mary Wanamaker was concerned not only about Thomas's attitude toward the Sabbath, but also about his unwillingness to abide by some of the behavioral principles taught at his father's Sunday School. She loved her son very much and suggested in many letters to him that he change some of his habits.

Shortly after the turn of the century and during the major rebuilding of the Philadelphia store, Thomas's health broke. Though he fought valiantly to maintain his leadership responsibilities at the store, it became physically impossible.

Reluctantly he informed his father that he could no longer continue in business. Resigning, he took an extended vacation to Africa and Europe only to be faced with increasing illness while overseas. Telegrams and letters arrived daily telling of Thomas's physical deterioration. John Wanamaker's entries in his diary reveal the agony of his heart as each day the news got worse. On March 2, 1908 Thomas B. Wanamaker died in Paris. His father, saddened and distraught, went away for a few days respite and wrote, "I have stopped here unable to settle myself to seeing people and undertaking my work."

Death in the immediate family was not a new experience for Mary and John. Their son Horace died in infancy in 1864, and their third child

Hattie, born in 1865, lived only five years. She seemed to possess an understanding and joy of life that endeared her to her parents in a more than usual fashion. They never quite reconciled themselves to her death.

LINDENHURST

As her husband's business grew and the family increased, activities at home more than doubled for Mary. She was not only a busy mother but also the gracious hostess for innumerable family friends, members of Bethany, her husband's business associates and distinguished religious, political and military leaders ranging from D. L. Moody, Billy Sunday, and General Pershing to President Benjamin Harrison.

The family lived for a while at 1336 Walnut Street in Philadelphia and then at 2032 Walnut, which they called "their City home." They spent the spring and autumn months at "Lindenhurst," a sprawling 108-acre country estate in Jenkintown, a northern suburb.

Early in his business career when he was but thirty years old, Wanamaker purchased this old country home on land originally owned by Billy Penn. Washington's troops had marched through the grounds and skirmished against the King's army using the old home as an outpost. Some years later in 1880, Wanamaker replaced the house with a large, Queen-Anne-style home built of grey stone quarried on the grounds and added a rich red-tile roof. Mrs. Wanamaker took personal charge of the house, the velvety lawns and the gardens filled with flowers of all kinds surrounding a reflecting pool and an artificial lake below the house. Nearby was another cottage where John's mother lived until her death in 1881. The estate included large stables and sheep houses, coachmen's and gardeners' houses, conservatories for the growing of plants and flowers and a dairy house built over natural springs. A workable 500-acre farm was farther up Old York Road.

For the enjoyment of their daughters, the Wanamakers built a fully equipped playhouse, "The Bird's Nest," on a wooded slope nearby. It was a two-story house in miniature, "just like the grown-ups," and contained several rooms, an upstairs covered porch, a back porch, and a fireplace. There were all the conveniences of home. Yet another stone building included an indoor swimming pool, an upstairs billiard room, and a bowling alley added in 1889.

A favorite pastime for the girls and the whole family was horseback

Lindenhurst, 1910

riding around the estate. At other times they enjoyed sitting at the edge of the reflecting pool filled with lilies and guarded by two large stone lions.

Though a huge iron fence with an imposing entrance gate encircled the estate, there was no high wall for secrecy. Wanamaker said, "I wish to share all these things with others who have less." Open house was normal at Lindenhurst. Whenever the Men's Brotherhood or the Roman Legion of Bethany came for their annual family picnics, Wanamaker, though still dressed in his coat, vest and black bow-tie, would roll up the cuffs of his pants and become the jovial, laughing, congenial host, playing lawn games and making everyone around him happy.

Mrs. Wanamaker loved it too. She called her home "an elastic house." After a very busy weekend of entertaining she wrote:

> I had a family of 28 for 4 days; now I have only 20. When all other help meets fail, I am sure that I shall be able to keep a boarding house. [9]

The Bungalow on the estate was a smaller home where Mr. Wanamaker preferred to stay when the rest of the family was away on vacations in the mountains of New York, at the beaches of New Jersey or traveling about England or Europe. He enjoyed the quiet solace and beauty that surrounded him as he watched squirrels darting about for food or listened to the birds singing their early morning songs. After his Bible reading and morning prayers at the breakfast table with family members or just a servant, a brisk early morning walk provided sufficient inspiration to last him throughout the day. At other times, he, like the other members of the family, enjoyed a horseback ride around the estate or through neighboring fields.

Following a tragic fire that totally destroyed the main house in 1907, Rodman Wanamaker built an even more luxurious 300-room French-styled mansion for his parents, complete with music room and art gallery for the large collection of art that he and his father had purchased at the Paris Salon. It was there in the magnificent mansion with its sprawling lawns and gardens that Mary Wanamaker lived until her death in 1920, a faithful and loving wife for sixty years.

Though many of the wealthy chose to reside in nearby Chestnut Hill or the western suburbs on the popular "Main Line" in places like Bryn Mawr, Haverford, St. Davids and Wayne, it was typical of the Wanamakers to circumvent the usual social whirl of the affluent and remain where they had first established their home just eight years after they were married. They had good company with the likes of Edward T. Stotesbury, John B. Stetson, Jay Cooke, J. B. Lippincott and Lucretia Mott whose homes were also in the "Old York Road" area, along the famous old turnpike. Later on they were joined by Widener, Elkins, and Cyrus Curtis.

THE WANAMAKER DAUGHTERS

JOHN AND MARY WANAMAKER HAD TWO DAUGHTERS who survived childhood but neither was expected to step into the family business at the death of their oldest brother, Thomas. Women in those days, at least those with wealth, were not involved in the business world. Mary (Minnie) and Elizabeth (Lillie), unlike their parents, enjoyed the social whirl and both married quite well.

Lillie Wanamaker, born in 1876, became the wife of Norman M. McLeod on June 6, 1900. A graduate of the University of Pennsylvania, McLeod served as an officer in the Spanish-American War and was assistant plant director of the Emergency Fleet Corporation during World War I. He became a prominent stockbroker, establishing his own firm as a member of the New York Stock Exchange. He was associated with the *Philadelphia Evening Telegraph* and became a member of many clubs. Lillie, a member of Bethany Church, was noted for her deeds as a worker during World War I. She served as Director of the Women's Liberty Loan Committee and was an active participant on the War Relief Committee of Emergency Aid. Both she and her husband were active in the social life of Philadelphia until her death in 1927. They did not have children.

Minnie Wanamaker, born in 1871, married Barclay Harding Warburton on June 13, 1895. Warburton, publisher of the *Evening Telegraph* and a military attache at the United States Embassy in London during World War I, was Philadelphia's Director of Welfare. He was appointed Police Commissioner of Philadelphia and later became Mayor of Palm Beach, Florida.

Mrs. Warburton became distinguished as a leader in welfare work and politics. She helped organize the Emergency Aid Fund of Pennsylvania and later served as President; was a founder of the Council of Republican Women of Pennsylvania; was appointed the First Woman Vice-Chairman of the Republican State Committee in 1920 and four years later became the first woman to serve as a member of the Pennsylvania State Republican National Committee. She was the first woman member of the Board of Trustees of Temple University and also served on the Board of the Presbyterian Hospital [her father had been one of the founders, her mother one of the benefactors, and her brother Thomas, a trustee]. Whereas her mother contributed considerable amounts of money to many welfare and non-profit organizations, Mary Warburton went a step further and became a participant in numerous organizations such as the Pennsylvania Women's Advisory Committee for the New York World's Fair in 1939. The mother of three children she died in 1954 at the age of eighty-five. She lived one year longer than her father.

LOUIS RODMAN WANAMAKER

EVERYONE WHO KNOWS EVEN A LITTLE BIT about the Wanamaker stores during the first quarter of the twentieth century also knows of Louis Rodman Wanamaker, the youngest son of John and Mary, born in 1863. He, like his brother Thomas, attended Princeton, graduated in 1886 with an A.B. and in 1902 was awarded the M.A. degree. Having fallen in love with France during a family trip to Europe in 1875, it was easy for him

The "Birds Nest" playhouse for the Wanamaker daughters, Lindenhurst, 1888

Reflecting Pool, Lindenhurst, 1910

with his new bride, Fernanda Henry, to take up residence in 1888 in Paris as the primary buyer of European goods for the Philadelphia store. Remaining there for ten years, he acquired knowledge of the finest French goods available and became greatly responsible for the artistic creations and cultural developments of the John Wanamaker stores in both Philadelphia and New York.

Diligent, hard-working and never one to rest on his father's financial laurels, Rodman caught his father's vision of a businessman's responsibility to serve the general public beyond the sale of dependable, fair-priced goods. Never minimizing the advantages of wealth, he, nevertheless, had no patience with frivolity, sometimes a characteristic of the rich. Referring to some family members vacationing in Scotland, he expressed his concern to his sister Minnie:

> I am just hoping it will give them renewed health and strength, and the opportunity of some quietness that their thoughts will be more serious and their consciences will realize there is much more in life than personal gratification. [10]

Rodman Wanamaker, son of John Wanamaker

No two adults ever agreed so much on so many things as Rodman Wanamaker and his father John. The love and respect that each had for the other is utterly astonishing. "My Dear and Precious Rodman," wrote John, "I am generous enough to wish that every man had a son as thoughtful and good to his father." [11]

Shortly after John died, Rodman, at age sixty, said, "It is my greatest desire to carry out what I know was the uppermost wish of the Founder." He also instructed his father's biographer that all the enterprise and innovations that had to do with the business and were introduced during his father's lifetime were "to be credited by the biographer to John Wanamaker." Rodman was content to live in his father's shadow.

A LOVER OF ART AND MUSIC

AT AN EARLY AGE, RODMAN BECAME AWARE of his father's love of art. So when he lived in Europe, he, too, began to acquire paintings that were sent home to the store where they would be hung for public viewing. In 1893 he purchased Pierre Fritel's "Les Conquerants," which he had seen at the Paris Salon the preceding year. A huge canvas, 16' high and 27' wide, it was a tragic picture of the horrible results of famous but ruthless military conquerors of past generations. In the foreground are Rameses II, Attila the Hun, Hannibal, Julius Caesar, Napoleon and others, all in full military regalia, on horseback, riding a corridor between rows of the fallen naked bodies of their victims. Rodman titled it "A Picture That Pleads The Cause Of Peace." Thousands of people flocked to the store to see this much-heralded painting, just one of hundreds of paintings that could be seen in the Art Galleries located on the seventh and eighth floors in Wanamaker's Philadelphia store. It was sold in 1988.

In similar fashion, Rodman advanced his father's appreciation for music. His father asked, "Why can't we bring more music into the lives of people?" Even in the early days when the store was housed in the old Pennsylvania Railroad Freight Depot, a small organ was purchased and placed conspicuously for employees and customers alike to enjoy. Everyone gathered round for the singing of familiar melodies at the opening and closing of the store each day.

When Rodman returned from a trip to Europe in 1910 during the construction of the new store in Philadelphia, he suggested that the finest organ in the world be built for the Grand Court, which his father later referred to as a "Temple." The complete story of the Wanamaker Organ, which was originally a part of the St. Louis World's Fair in 1904, is found in another chapter of this book.

Bringing to the Grand Court the world's greatest organists was only part of Rodman's plan to provide Philadelphians with fine music gratuitously. Possessing a keen interest in violins and other stringed instruments, he sought the assistance of musical experts as he began to collect rare Italian violins, violas, cellos and basses which were not to be placed in museum cases but played by distinguished artists in public concerts at the store. Only the best concert halls entertained so many world-renowned musicians as those who performed in the Philadelphia and New York Wanamaker stores.

THE NEW YORK STORE

EARLIER, WHILE RODMAN WAS STILL IN EUROPE IN 1896, his father purchased the A.T. Stewart department store in New York City. It had enjoyed a very favorable reputation while Stewart was living but had rapidly declined following his death. Initially Wanamaker sent Robert C. Ogden, his trusted business associate, to be resident-partner. But in 1900 Rodman returned from France following the death of his wife when she was only thirty-six. Distraught and extremely sorrowful, he found a new challenge as his father sent him to the New York store to assist Ogden. John rewarded him well for his labors. He wrote:

> You had better have a fixed salary of $25,000 per month and one per-cent on growth increase of sales over 1906.[12]

When Ogden reached the age of retirement in 1907, Rodman succeeded him, became a partner with his father, and was given seemingly unrestrictive freedom in further developing the store. Someone said, "John Wanamaker filled Rodman's pockets with money every morning and let him loose." It must be remembered, however, that John Wanamaker, as long as he lived, was the sole owner of his business, the inventory and the real estate. He answered to no one except himself. He made decisions on the moment without the necessity of committee or board approval. The partnership that he formed with his sons, with

Ogden and a few others was a partnership for profits only. Even though he was willing to share his success with those who helped attain it, he was not going to risk ultimate decisions with anyone, not even his sons. He wrote to Rodman:

> It is my purpose that you shall have the executive management of the New York business, subject only to myself. [13]

With consummate skill, boundless energy and the unflagging confidence of his father, Rodman lifted the New York Store to new heights. The guiding genius was his father, but that fact takes no credit away from Rodman who caught the vision of the Wanamaker principles of business where merchandise had to be first quality. In New York, style seemed as important as quality merchandise, and Rodman brought impressive credentials to his job.

Having learned fashion and design while in Paris where he was President of the American Art Foundation, Rodman creatively inspired the manufacture of new weaves, designs and fashions in America. Living in New York amidst the affluent, he catered to their taste for the finest while at the same time introducing a more conservative simplicity of appearance. He possessed a rare combination of management skills and artistic genius.

Referred to as "an artist in business," he fashioned his store unlike any other: "A gallery of art and fashion; a studio where all might learn." He strongly believed that when people lived in a home environment of beauty, they were apt to have peace, harmony and contentment in their own lives. Aesthetics were as important to him as the quality of the merchandise he sold.

As in the Philadelphia store, the architectural design of the New York store was a natural attraction for the public. Rodman capitalized upon it. Musical programs equal in quality and prestige of performance to any found within the city were offered regularly, without cost to the public.

As a thorough, hard-working businessman, he was not happy when the Philadelphia store sales exceeded his in New York. He and his father in Philadelphia, compared daily sales and developed a friendly, competitive spirit, with the father chiding the son when sales lagged behind:

> I wonder why you are not selling as many domestic rugs as we are....We sold l85-9'x 12's yesterday.[14]

After the death of his father in 1922, Rodman became the sole owner of both the Philadelphia and New York stores, spending three days each week in both cities. His secretary traveled back and forth with him by train as he poured over correspondence and various reports. Records show that under his leadership annual sales reached their highest level in the history of the business prior to the Great Depression of the 1930s.

A PUBLIC SERVANT

FOLLOWING IN THE STEPS OF HIS FATHER, Rodman became as well-known to the New York public as his father was in the City of Brotherly Love. He took an interest in public affairs and was appointed Special Deputy Police Commissioner as the Mayor's official greeter of distinguished guests from around the world. Often he was referred to as "The Millionaire Cop." He was frequently photographed with kings and queens, presidents and premiers, cardinals and generals sitting with him in his car. It was said that Rodman's 1914 Landaulette Rolls Royce was made famous by the many world-wide dignitaries it had carried.

Rodman had a flair for publicity that was unique and subtly commercial. Blending a genuine interest in history, patriotism, scientific progress and religion, he spent millions of his own money in public-service ventures that kept the Wanamaker name and business in the headlines. To mention but a few, there was the fifteenth-century-style silver altar that he gave to St. Mark's Episcopal Church in Philadelphia in memory of his wife Fernanda Henry. It has been described as "the greatest work of ecclesiastical art in twentieth century America." When King Edward of England saw it, he was so impressed that Wanamaker had a duplicate made for the Royal Chapel, in the King's honor.

Rodman also, in 1922, presented Westminster Abbey with an eight-foot-high ivory and gold Cross adorned with sapphires and diamonds which has since been carried at the head of the procession for coronations, royal weddings, funerals and affairs of state in England.

Shortly after the turn of the century, the plight of the American Indian became a concern of many. Often referred to as "The Vanishing Race," the Indians lived restricted lives on government reservations and were treated as oddities. Desiring to preserve a record of their valuable heritage, Rodman Wanamaker financed three educational expositions to the West from 1908 to 1913 and secured numerous photographs of

Indian life, a priceless documentary today. The Smithsonian Institution in Washington, the Indiana State University Museum, the American Museum of Natural History in New York City, and several other institutions possess thousands of photographs, glass negatives and glass lantern slides of Indians in their natural habitat, the result of this venture.

He also proposed that a National American Indian Memorial be built at his expense at Fort Wordsworth on Staten Island in New York Harbor. Though authorized by an act of the United States Congress in 1911 and given personal attention by President Taft who visited the site for the official "inauguration" ceremonies on February 22, 1913, the effort never materialized. It seems that a combination of problems leading up to World War I and reported controversy within the Bureau of Indian Affairs at the time were obstacles too great to overcome.

WANAMAKER-MILLROSE GAMES

IN 1908, RODMAN INITIATED THE WANAMAKER-MILLROSE GAMES, the widely known and most prestigious indoor track and field event in the world. Aimed "to inspire, to improve, and to promote American amateur athletics" and chartered in 1910, they initially provided recreational opportunities for the Wanamaker employees. Later on, the Games were opened to everyone and have attracted athletes from more than two dozen foreign countries. Many Millrose contestants, like Cornelius Warmerdam, Glenn Cunningham, Gil Dodds, John Thomas, Gunnar Nielsen, Carl Lewis and Mary Decker, established new world records. Many became Olympic gold or silver medalists. The Games continue to be held each year at Madison Square Garden in New York but are now financed by other commercial organizations.

A PIONEER IN AERONAUTICS

RODMAN WANAMAKER WAS DEEPLY INTERESTED in the development of air transportation. He invested millions of dollars in the construction of "America," which he intended to be the first flying boat to make a trans-Atlantic flight. An avid promoter of commercial aviation, he wrote in 1914 to the Aero Club of America:

In the cause of Science and in the interest of world peace, I have the honor to announce my intention to make a purely scientific test of areo-nautic power by crossing the Atlantic Ocean in one flight if possible. The crossing of the Atlantic Ocean in one flight of an aircraft is, to my mind, as important to aerial navigation as was the voyage of Columbus to transportation by water. It will be of far more practical importance than was the successful expedition to the North Pole. [15]

Constructed by Glenn Curtis, the "America" was ready for the trans-Atlantic flight in the summer of 1914, but World War I disrupted plans

and Rodman Wanamaker put the plane at the disposal of the United States government. Finally, thirteen years later, on June 30, 1927, the third model of "America" completed its non-stop 4,200 mile flight from New York to Ver-sur-Mer on the Brittany coast of France. Commander Richard E. Byrd, and his crew of three, successfully made the first crossing of the Atlantic in a tri-motor plane, just a month after Charles Lindbergh made his epic solo flight in his single-motored "Spirit of St Louis."

Patriotism had been instilled in young Wanamaker while he still lived at home with his parents. Possessing a genuine love for his country, Rodman, like his father, felt indebted to a land that provided opportunity for them to develop their dreams. During World War I, the two of them purchased more War Bonds than anyone else in the nation and virtually placed their enormous wealth at the disposal of the government. Rodman's Coat of Arms, painstakingly fashioned, bore the words, "Ubique Patriam Reminisci," which translated means "To Remember Your Country Everywhere." At the close of the War, he was appointed head of the Mayor's Committee to welcome home troops arriving in New York harbor, and he also personally financed and presented to New York City the "Eternal Light Monument" at Madison Square as a memorial honoring the city's war dead.

When Rodman Wanamaker died in 1928, the *New York Times* gave him front page coverage and referred to him as "Merchant, Art Patron, and Sponsor of Aviation." President Coolidge called him "a merchant of high ideals who lavishly gave of his means and time to public enterprises and private philanthropies." Words of sorrow at his death and praise for his endeavors filled the newspapers.

Attending the funeral service in Philadelphia were more than 150 distinguished and prominent persons from New York, including Mayor Walker, who arrived on a special train consisting of several pullman and dining cars. At St. Mark's Episcopal Church, the service, similar to most funerals, also included organ and violin music, his favorite.

Dr. Thaddeus Rich, Concert-master of the Philadelphia Orchestra played "The Swan," the last violin made by Stradivarius, which Wanamaker had purchased for his string collection.

Rodman Wanamaker was buried in the crypt with his father, mother and other family members in the Wanamaker Bell Tower mausoleum in St. James the Less Episcopal Cemetery in Philadelphia.

During the summer that followed his death, France honored its long-time friend by sending three distinguished French journalists to present a bronze urn to be placed in his tomb. It contained earth from three places in France associated with American history: the grave of Lafayette at Picus cemetery in Paris; the spot where the first Americans fell in the World War near Luneville; and Ver-sur Mer, where Commander Byrd had landed the Wanamaker sponsored airplane, "America."

With his death a most unique era in American business history had come to an end.

> "Rodman Wanamaker was the greatest symbol of the spirit of Washington and of Lafayette. He was one of the greatest intelligences of the United States. He was a great citizen, a noble leader in everything, a great man and a great father to humanity, filled with idealism, duty and love."
> Dr. Marcel Knecht, French-American
> Committee of the French Press.[16]

THE SEQUEL TO LINDENHURST

LINDENHURST, SO NAMED BECAUSE OF THE LARGE NUMBER of Linden trees, was located at 8300 Old York Road in Chelten Hills, Pa., at the intersection of Townshipline Road (Route 73), just ten miles from central Philadelphia.

Following the deaths of Mary and John Wanamaker and their son Rodman, the French Renaissance-style mansion and 81 acre estate was purchased by Henry W. Breyer and his wife, neighbors of the Wanamakers. Unfortunately, it fell into disrepair during the great depression. In 1944, Henry W. Breyer, Jr. bought the estate as a gift for the Philadelphia Council of the Boy Scouts of America for a scout training area and wildlife refuge. During the 1980s it was sold to Breyer Associates who have developed this historic site for condominiums, townhouses, and an office building. The original Wanamaker iron lattice-work, domed gazebeo and stone bridge have been preserved—a favorite site for wedding photos.

A Genealogical Survey

JOHN WANAMAKER'S PATERNAL ANCESTORS lived in the Rhineland-Palitinate area of Germany, and immigrated to America in the middle of the eighteenth century between 1731 and 1756. George Wannemacher's first home was in Northampton County, Pennsylvania.

Henry Wannemacher, John's great-grandfather, moved from his parents' home in Pennsylvania about 1791 and settled on a farm in Huntingdon County, New Jersey, on the banks of the Delaware River just above Trenton. Geographically, it was similar to the valleys and hills of their German homeland. During the time of the American Revolution, Henry joined other young men of the area in taking up arms in the fight for independence. His father hauled military supplies to the battlefront.

John Wanamaker, one of Henry's six children, moved to Ohio near Dayton along the Miami River between 1810 and 1820. He changed the spelling of his name from Wannemacher to Wanamaker. His wife, Anna Hann, bore five children and died while young, leaving behind a sorrowing and lonely husband. Abandoning his promising trade as a builder, John moved back east to Philadelphia, established a new business as a brickmaker, and married Elizabeth Hurst Locke in 1833. Following the birth of two more children he moved to Leesburg, Indiana with his second family.

Nelson Wanamaker, John's second son, was born in 1811. He continued in the brickmaking business in South Philadelphia and married Elizabeth Deshong Kochersperger, the daughter of a nearby innkeeper. Both of her parents were descendants of French Huguenots who had immigrated directly to Penn's colony in the preceding century.

The first-born child of Nelson and Elizabeth Wanamaker was a son whom they named John after his paternal grandfather. Born on July 11, 1838 in their humble home near Gray's Ferry, he became a man of honor, prestige, fame and influence in the business world, the halls of government and politics, and in civil affairs and religious organizations.

THOUGH THIS WRITER HAS COMPILED a more detailed genealogical listing of the Wanamaker family than seen here, the information given below seems to be adequate for the purpose and intent of this book. It is presented in simple form for quick reference.

GREAT-GREAT-GRANDFATHER—
> **George Wannemacher** (1718-1795) of Lehigh Twp.,
> > Northampton County, Pa.
> > Married—Elizabeth Catherina
> > Children—Peter, Regina Muffley, Anna Margaretha Leibengut, Maria Elizabeth Solt, Christina Ohl, Johanetta Ross, Catharina, Henry and Elizabetha

GREAT-GRANDFATHER—
> **Henry (Heinrich) Wannemacher** (1753-1831)
> > Married—Maria (Mary)—D-1822
> > Children—
> > > Suzanna (Neas)—1782
> > > John—1787-1851
> > > Nicholas —1791
> > > George—1799
> > > Mary (Smith)
> > > Hannah (Gaddis) D-1822

GRANDFATHER—
> **John Wanamaker** (1787-1851)
> > Married—Anna Hahn
> > Married—Elizabeth Hurst Locke—1798-1877
> > Children—
> > > Samuel R.—about 1810
> > > Nelson—1811-1862
> > > Wilson—1814
> > > George—1819
> > > Mary Ann
> > > John Wesley—1834
> > > Susannah—1837

FATHER—
> **Nelson Wanamaker**—(1811-1862)
>> Married—Elizabeth Deshong Kochersperger—1818-1888
>> Children—
>>> John—1838-1922
>>> William Henry —1840-1905
>>> Elizabeth (Fry)—1842-1925
>>> Mary Ellen (Fales)—1845-1918
>>> Samuel M.—1847-1904
>>> Francis Marion—1850-1916
>>> Belle—1856-1859

THE FOUNDER—
> **John Wanamaker**—(1838-1922)
>> Married—Mary Brown—1839-1920
>> Children—
>>> Thomas Brown —1861-1908
>>> Lewis Rodman—1863-1928 (*)
>>> Horace—1864-1864
>>> Hattie—1865-1870
>>> Mary Brown (Warburton)—1871-1954
>>> Elizabeth (McLeod)—1876-1927

GRANDCHILDREN—
> Rodman Wanamaker, II
> Thomas B. Wanamaker, Jr.
> Fernanda Wanamaker Heeren Munn
> John Wanamaker, Jr. (Captain) (**)
> Marie Louise Wanamaker Munn Kent
> Barclay H. Warburton, Jr.
> Charles Egerton Warburton
> Mary Brown Warburton

GREAT-GRANDCHILDREN—
> Lynn Willing Wanamaker Rice
> Mary Wanamaker Watriss
> Alexandra Devereaux Wanamaker Gross
> Rodman Arturo Heeren
> John Rodman Wanamaker (***)

Fernanda Pauline Wanamaker Wetherill Leas
Fernanda Wanamaker Munn Kellogg
Gurnee Munn, Jr.
Rosemary Warburton Chisholm Gaynor
Barclay H. Warburton, 3rd
Anne Aldred Warburton Girvin
Mary Brown Warburton Boltron, 3rd
Wendy Warburton Clark

Note: Following the death of the Founder, his son Rodman (*) became the sole owner of the John Wanamaker business. Upon his death, the trustees of the estate managed the business in which the grandson, John Wanamaker, Jr. (**), was employed until his death in 1954. The last member of the family to be involved in the business was John Rodman Wanamaker (***), great-grandson of the Founder, who was chairman of the Board of Directors from 1955 to 1978.

Wanamaker family portrait, Christimas 1900

The Letters of Mary Wanamaker

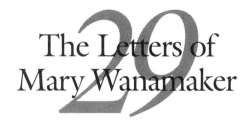

IN OUR DAY WHEN TELEPHONE CONVERSATIONS provide instant communication with family and friends, there is an unfortunate loss of recorded conversations found in letters and handwritten notes of an earlier generation. We have also lost the contemplative reflection and intimacy that occurs in exchanging letters. How will future historians document attitudes and affections of a generation that seldom writes to others or adds only a brief notation to a commercially printed greeting card?

Mary Wanamaker, born before the advent of the telephone, learned early to express her deepest feelings, as well as her thoughts, in simple and plain language in her letters. With servants at her side, her messages were delivered instantly to her husband or sons in their offices, to the homes of her children, and even to their rooms in the Wanamaker mansion when they were visiting or expected home. Even her notes to the servants characterize this remarkable woman so seldom in the public eye, but whose presence dominated the behind-the-scenes life of the Wanamaker family. Though the Wanamakers were among the first to acquire telephones, Mary never gave up her letter-writing.

Apparently John Wanamaker and his son Rodman sensed the significance of preserving a record of their lives for the benefit of their descendants or others, for it seems that very little was discarded. When Mary wrote to them while they were out of state or out of the country, her letters were read and then sent to the store to be placed in the office files.

With a desire to show the wholesome, caring and encouraging relationship of a loving mother, some of Mary Wanamaker's intimate letters to her son, Rodman, are printed here. Obviously, space does not permit more than a sampling, but that will be enough to catch her spirit. The following letters were written when Rodman was past forty years of age, married and the father of three children.[1]

****

Mary Wanamaker's Letter to Rodman on New Year's Eve.

I thank you beyond expression, Dear Darling Boy, for all the joy and happiness that you have given me all through the year that is fast leaving. I thank God that I can go with you through the Portals of the New One. The bells will soon be singing. Some are glad to part with the old one; some sorry.

"O Tender Christ, bless thou this coming year.
Bless thou its dawn and bless its noontide and its evening to my Beloved Boy.
May the brave things thought or spoken,
By the true deeds simply done,
By the mean things crushed and conquered,
And the bloodless battles won,
Send thy blessing on My Son."

Goodnight Darling and a Blessed good New Year.
Mother

****

Roddie, Dear Beloved,
Your sweet letters come as balm to the soul.
Mother

****

February 13, 1913

Dear Blessed Boy,
This is your birthday. On the calendar of those who know you, it is marked with gold. As both a Holy and a Holiday, you make us happy and you make us glad.
Mother

John and Mary Wanamaker, 1918

* * * * * * * * * *

Goodnight Angel Mine,
I hope your rest will be sweet.
    Your own devoted Mother. 1913

* * * * * * * * * *

I am praying day and night for your guardian angels to watch and guide
more closely and bring the Divine Peace that is yours.
    Your dear Mother - 1918

* * * * * * * * * *

Roddie Dear,
The week will be long without you.

* * * * * * * * * *

There are smiles that make me happy.
There are smiles that make me glad.
There are tears that come from sorrow.
There are tears that make one glad.
    Does the little parody convey to you Darling, some of my thoughts?
If the fairies were not extinct, I should imagine they come to see what my
boy could do next. They all come with joy.
    1918

* * * * * * * * * *

Roddie Love:
    A little boy went to Sunday School. On his return his Mother asked
him what he had learned. The little fellow said "about a man Enoch."
    His Mother questioned him further and learned from his baby lips
that a good man named Enoch went out one day to take a walk with God
and never came back.
    It is only the very, very good that may expect such an end to a beau-
tiful, unselfish life. I wonder why I told you this?
Your own happy loving Mother
    1918

* * * * * * * * * *

My whole soul whispers God bless you. The sweet incense of your dear faithful love followed me through the night and now goes on with the day.
Mother

* * * * * * * * * *

The care and thought you have given your old and young Mother have been marvelous. How could I inspire such affection in a boy? So undeserving. If the game of tenth were played, you would have ten to your credit every time and I not one!
Mother

* * * * * * * * * *

Happy is the Mother who can rest content that her Boy has learned the things which belong to His Peace.
1910

* * * * * * * * * *

I kiss you a thousand times, as deeply and fondly as I love you. I find my joy and happiness in being loved by you today, my dear precious Boy.
February 13th, 1905.

Mary Wanamaker's three-letter monogram

The Log College

President Benjamin Harrison Visits Lindenhurst

ONE OF AMERICA'S EARLIEST EDUCATIONAL INSTITUTIONS was the Log College at Neshaminy, Pennsylvania, founded by William Tennent in 1726. It was the first theological school in North America, predating the new nation.

At a special anniversary celebration of the college on September 5, 1889, President Benjamin Harrison was the honored guest. Arriving from Washington the day before, the President stayed at Lindenhurst, the nearby estate of John Wanamaker in Jenkintown. There he planted a small oak tree—symbolic of Wanamaker's first store, Oak Hall. The next morning, the President and Wanamaker, Postmaster General of the United States, entered their carriage for the short but dramatic journey to the ceremonial grounds at Neshaminy.

As they proceeded along Old York Road, more than 1500 hundred carriages followed. The road was lined with thousands of onlookers who had decorated trees, fences, and telegraph poles with red, white and blue national banners and flags. The forty-two piece band of the First Regiment of Philadelphia, dressed in scarlet uniforms, provided music. As the celebrities passed the Abington Presbyterian Church, they were greeted by 300 young children, each waving an American flag.

Passing under a huge sixty-foot wide arch, they stopped in front of the grandstand accommodating 700 distinguished, fancily dressed ladies. Flowers were presented to the women in the presidential party, including Mrs. Harrison who rode in the Governor's carriage with Mrs. Wanamaker, accompanied by Rev. Dr. Samuel Lowrie, the Wanamakers' personal friend and first minister of Bethany Presbyterian Church. Twenty-five thousand people had gathered to greet their President as he delivered his address at this memorable event.

John Wanamaker was also asked to speak. His address, given below, is illustrative of his natural talent to capture the significance of a special event, mark it with historic consequence, and stir the hearts of the audience with carefully selected words, phrases and illustrations. And always, there seemed to be in his mind a religious foundation for the things of life that have value.

JOHN WANAMAKER'S SPEECH

MR. CHAIRMAN AND FRIENDS—It is because I am your neighbor that I am honored today with a place on the program. Three months ago when my old and dear friend, the Rev. Dr. Murphy invited me to make an address, I said "No," but that I would endeavor to attend but not to speak.

Nevertheless, the compliment is paid by your committee to me of putting my name on your historic program which in itself is a roll of honor.

I am too grateful to take advantage of this by a long speech. Permit me to say that I share with you a pride of the good fortune that fixes our homes close to the revolutionary glories of Independence Hall and nearby the scenes of Germantown, Valley Forge and Neshaminy where the Log College makes its mark in the history of our nation.

A lowly spot this seems, to be the birthplace of the momentous movement that set in motion the early educational life of the land. But it is not the first time that out of obscure places, streams of light have shed brightness over the land—never more so than when the star shone on humble Bethlehem plains and the Light of the World came with angelic songs.

Centuries before, David came from Ramah's hidden pastures with a harp whose melody for 3000 years has been singing on.

In later days Elisha left the plough for that first school of the prophets of which the Log College was the successor. When those untitled heroes, in whose ancestry some of you may well be proud, came a century ago to this place to lay foundations for their College, their path lay through the shining gateway of faith in God. The bush that flamed at Moses' feet, indicating God's presence with His servants, must have glowed again before their reverent eyes.

Not in their own strength they came, neither were they alone. For Joshua and Elijah spoke again through those early teachers Isaiah and David and with lofty inspiration repeated their message. The apostles and martyrs took up the strain and the work of God had free course. He was glorified in the wide-spread beneficence of the institutions of learning that grew out of this holy ministry. For in number—not powerful or rich—without stone or costly carvings—they built a great cathedral, enduring as the truth of base and buttresses, columns and capstone, in itself a benediction to all the land. Created not by act of Parliament nor fostered by act of Congress, but in simple and strong confidence in the God whose Spirit led them, they wrought this work that will for the ages to come continue to manifest the wisdom and goodness of its founders and give glory to God.

I like the Memorial Day that places flowers on the graves of the nation's heroes. And I like the thought that gathers us to keep this feast of Celebration for the heroes of our faith. We stand together today on this high level, looking off over the centuries at the true men, whose work built the institutions we are now enjoying, while there comes to me, like the song of the nightingale, an inspiration that out of other humble places, true men may come up with God's blessing to do service, in the Church and State, for themselves and coming generations, for which the world will rise up and call them blessed. [1]

31

Honoring Temple University Founder Russell H. Conwell

****

Address By Honorable John Wanamaker

on the occasion of

Reverend Dr. Russell H. Conwell's

5000th delivery of his lecture

"ACRES OF DIAMONDS"

in the

Academy of Music

Philadelphia, Pa.

May 21, 1914

****

BORN IN PENNSYLVANIA AND PROUD OF MY CITY AND STATE I have always lived in, I am unable to find any other citizen that ranks above or who is the equal of Russell H. Conwell.

A poor Baptist minister he was fifty years ago—not a poor minister, mind you, but a brave, strong, hopeful soul who realized the world's poverty in its lack of means of education for its growing youth, and its consequences that condemned them to hard labor and a life of slender opportunities.

As the years came on, he saw thousands rising to manhood, whose careers became narrowed to little above physical labor. The low wages and lack of skill shut them off from being home-makers and compelled them to endure lives of loneliness and hopelessness.

But a great vision shone across his way in those days, when half the youth of the city could not be admitted to the schools, and before the public night schools were established.

Then it was that Russell H. Conwell, one overworked man, without means and standing almost alone, turned his church into a school for young men. Little by little it grew, and the struggling Pastor grew in faith and power; and thrown upon his own resources, he persuaded his congregation to do without him from Mondays to Saturdays. During the weeks, year after year, spending in the main only his Sundays with his Church people, he dealt in acres of diamonds and with them he built and maintained the great Temple College.

Those who have figured it out are my authority for stating to you, the product of the lectures of half a century, amount with interest compounded, to over eight millions of gold dollars. The part coming to Dr. Conwell he bestowed upon his heroic child, the Temple College, and the other portion of the proceeds going to the various schools, charities and churches in whose interest the lectures were given.

If there is another man in the State of Pennsylvania that has done as much for his State as Dr. Conwell, I cannot name him.

Where is there another one man who has in his lifetime given the opportunity to 40,000 men to get an education?

Ask the men of this city and those scattered all over the United States, in Japan, China, Philippines, Hawaii.

Ask the fellows in the Army, and Navy, on the Mexican Border, standing at their posts with their guns in hand.

Ask them all who their greatest benefactor was, and with a mighty shout that will reach the stars and the God of Heaven above them, they will shout, "Russell H. Conwell;" the man who battled on through storm and strife, in poverty and sickness, in darkness and disappointment, with unfailing hope and courage, battered, never beaten, the mighty-souled lover of his kind, Russell H. Conwell.

Philadelphia honors herself tonight in honoring Russell H. Conwell, who has shared his life. And now, he comes to bring you "Acres of Diamonds."[1]

John Wanamaker: Activist

During the last year of John Wanamaker's life when he was 84 years of age, the listing below was prepared to indicate the broad scope of his involvement in religious and community affairs both locally and nationally.

It must be kept in mind that if his philanthropic endeavors were also included, the list would indeed be much longer. It is repeated here just as it was written in 1922.

Mr John Wanamaker is a member of the General Assembly of the Presbyterian Church, Vice-Moderator of the Presbytery of Philadelphia, and Senior Elder of the Bethany Collegiate Presbyterian Church, being the active Superintendent of the Sunday School since he founded it in 1858.

Mr. Wanamaker is a 33rd degree Mason, being a member of the Friendship Lodge 400, Jenkintown, Abington Chapter and Mary Commandery, Philadelphia Consistory,

President of the World's Sunday School Association,

President of the Board of Trustees of the Pennsylvania State Sabbath School Association,

President of First Penny Savings Bank of Philadelphia,

President of the Board of Trustees of the Williamson Free School of Mechanical Trades,

President of the Board of Trustees of the Wanamaker Institute of Industries,

President of the Bethany Brotherhood of Andrew and Philip,

President of the Men's Friendly Union, John Chambers Church,

A member of the Board of Public Education of Philadelphia,

A member of the Philadelphia Art Jury, Vice President,

A member of the Pennsylvania Academy of the Fine Arts,

And a member of the following organizations:

> American Star Lodge, No. 405, I.O.O.F.
> Grand Lodge, F. & A.M.
> Chairman, Masonic Library Committee
> The Union League of Philadelphia
> The Art Club
> The Manufacturers Club
> Moses Lodge, No. 66, L.P. of A.
> Young Republicans of Philadelphia
> French Legion of Honor
> Presbyterian Social Union
> National Institute of Social Science
> The Franklin Institute
> Audubon Society
> Presbyterian Superintendents Association
> Pennsylvania-German Society
> Pennsylvania Museum & School of Industrial Art
> American Academy of Political & Social Science
> Fairmount Park Art Association
> Union Society of the Civil War
> National Association for Study & Prevention of Tuberculosis
> Transatlantic Society of America
> George G. Meade Post No. 1
> Genealogical Society of Pennsylvania
> The Hampton Association

Boy Scouts of America
Pan-American Society of the United States
Religious Education Association
The Agassiz Association
Kensington Dispensary
Philadelphia Bible Society
National Masonic Research Society
Delaware Co. S. P. C. A.
Old York Road Fire Company
Jenkintown Improvement Association
American Economic Association
American Red Cross
Legal Aid Society
Apprentices Free Library
Metropolitan Museum of Art
Japan Society
The Penn Club
Public Education & Child Labor Association

General John J. Pershing, John Wanamaker, Colonel Hyatt—June 15, 1921
(The World War hero was awarded the Doctor of Military Science degree by Wanamaker,
President of the Board of Trustees of the Pennsylvania Military College, Chester, Pa.)

Civil Service Reform Association
Philadelphia Society for Promotion of Liberal Studies
City Club of Philadelphia
Pennsylvania Conservation Society
University of Pennsylvania Museum
Pennsylvania Arbitration & Peace Society
The German Society
The Economic Club
National Institute of Efficiency
Pennsylvania Forestry Association
Citizens Corps General U.S. Grant Post No. 5
Chamber of Commerce, New York
Chamber of Commerce, Philadelphia
Honorary Member, Chamber of Commerce, Atlantic City
Philadelphia Bourse
Historical Society of Pennsylvania
Pennsylvania Society Archaeological Institute of America
American Civic Alliance
Public Education Association
Friendly Sons of St. Patrick
Civil Service Reform Association
Philadelphia Sabbath Association
Presbyterian Orphanage
Presbyterian Elders Association
Huguenot Society
The Gideons-Christian Commission Travelers Association
     of America
North American Civic League for Immigrants
Philadelphia Board of Trade
Philadelphia Real Estate Board
Philadelphia Daily Vacation Bible School Association
Advisory Board, Presbyterian Home for Aged Couples
     and Single Men
Advisory Board, Presbyterian Orphanage
Valley Forge Historical Society
St. Petersburg Yacht Club
Brookline Square Club
Presbyterian Historical Society
Carlton Club of London [1]

"The only wish I have, is that I could have done my work better."

An Autobiographical Sketch

On the back of a used envelope cut in half and dated 1915, John Wanamaker, in his own handwriting summarized the important events and dates in his life. Never one to use adjectives to describe his own person, he simply stated the facts that the record might be kept straight. It is given here just as he wrote it that day.

JOHN WANAMAKER WAS BORN IN THE COUNTY OF PHILADELPHIA, before it was all taken into the city, in 1838. He was of Dutch and Huguenot ancestry, attended country school and went to work in 1852 in a book store. Afterward he was copyist and office boy in Attorney-at-Law, Nathaniel B. Brown's office, and then moved with his family to Indiana, where his grandfather lived, returned in 1855, and was employed in Bennett's Clothing Store.

Mr. Wanamaker established and edited *Everybody's Journal.*

He was elected the first paid secretary of the Young Men's Christian Association of Philadelphia, and assisted George H. Stuart in establishing it.

He was also one of the founders and first honorary secretary of the Christian Commission of the Civil War times.

In 1861 he established business on Market Street, Philadelphia.

In 1869 he was elected President of the Young Men's Christian Association, and later raised the money and built in Philadelphia the first great building of the Young Men's Christian Association, outside of New York. With the assistance of George W. Childs and A. J. Drexel he organized the Citizens' Relief Committee for relief in the Irish famine, which became afterwards the permanent Relief Committee.

He is President of the Pennsylvania State Sunday School Association, Incorporated, and is still Chairman of its Board of Trustees.

In 1875 he raised the first million dollars in stock subscriptions, cashed by the merchants and bankers of Philadelphia for the Centennial Board of Finance, was Chairman of the Board of Finance, operating the first great exhibition, and is the only member of that Board now living, of which John Welsh was President.

In 1875 he took over the Pennsylvania Railroad Freight Station and expanded and enlarged the business under a new system known as Americanized Retailing, which has spread over the world.

He established the *Farm Journal*, with Wilmer Atkinson as Editor, and owned and published *The Sunday School Times,* and brought to Philadelphia Henry Clay Trumbull, as Editor.

Mr. Wanamaker was an early member of the Union League, Committee of One Hundred, and active in public affairs.

With Professor Saunders he started, by subscriptions and otherwise, the Presbyterian Hospital, The Children's Ward being contributed from his family.

He was one of the founders of the Presbyterian Orphanage.

With William Pepper, then Provost of the University of Pennsylvania, he founded the Commercial Museum and aided the first steps of the Archaeological Museum in the collection and gift of Indian antiquities, and bronzes of Herculaneum and Pompeii.

In 1888 he was a member of the Electoral College, electing Benjamin Harrison, President.

In 1889 he was appointed Postmaster-General and served for four years. He established Sea Postal offices, Rural Free Delivery, aided in the abolition of Lottery by mail, wrote the first schedules and aided in establishing foreign mail services under which four steamships, now existing, came under the American flag. With Henniker Heston he advocated two-cent postage on sea and land.

He received the degree of L.L.D. from Howard University, Washington, D. C., and subsequently from Ursinus College, Collegeville, Penna., his home county. [Also the L.L.D. degree from the University of Pennsylvania in 1915.]

The degree of Chevalier of the Legion of Honor was conferred on him by the President of the French Republic, 1911.

He founded and chartered the University of Trade and Applied Commerce, which operates business schools of 600 students, begun 1878 with the first school stores.

He founded in 1870, and is President of the Bethany College, now the Wanamaker Institute of Industries, with pupils numbering last year 1253 young men and young women.

He founded the Bethany Presbyterian Church in 1858, the John Chambers Memorial Presbyterian Church in 1897, and the Bethany Temple Presbyterian Church in 1906.

He is Chairman of the Board of the Williamson Free School of Mechanical Trades, being a member selected by Isaiah V. Williamson.

He is also a member of the Board of Education of the City of Philadelphia.

He founded in 1888 the First Penny Savings Fund under a new act to protect depositors, which is now a general law. [1]

INDEPENDENCE HALL.
PHILADELPHIA.

To Labor and to Rest

IT MAY SEEM THAT JOHN WANAMAKER NEVER STOPPED WORKING and was what the present world calls a "workaholic." Not so. One of the strong personal characteristics that enabled him to accomplish so much and become so successful in life was his ability to rest and relax. At the end of a busy day he enjoyed solitary moments of quietness when he relaxed in the beauty of a sunset or in watching a rabbit scurry across his lawn.

He did not have nor did he need entertainment provided by the modern media of radio, television or even movies. The theater held no attraction for him and seldom did he visit the concert hall.

Riding horseback or enjoying a ride in his carriage or auto provided all the recreation he needed until he was in his seventies and became an avid fisherman. He spent several winters off the Florida Keys in the Gulf of Mexico on his 100-foot-long houseboat, and he participated in fishing contests while still dressed in his signature bow tie and vest. Always competitive, he fished as vigorously as he ran his business, winning prizes for the first kingfish caught in the new season and the largest number of fish caught in a single day. But throughout the year, apart from extended vacations, the tensions of his work schedule were relieved by casual reading, conversing with friends and in personally writing letters to family and friends. Though his burdens must often have been enormous, he never allowed his work to be a chore.

He chose capable people as chiefs in his stores and church and trained them to implement his policies and practices. He was then able to withdraw and relax with the confidence that all would go well even when he was absent.

Beginning in 1871 he made the first of his trips to Europe to purchase $50,000 worth of English woolens for his Chestnut Street store. [He said he crossed the ocean forty-four times.] But it was also a "working vacation." He was never content in making a trip totally work-cen-

John Wanamaker's cottage at Cape May Point, New Jersey

John Wanamaker at his cottage, 1890

tered or totally vacation. It had to be both. Sight-seeing, visiting famous historical places, meeting distinguished world leaders and attending various churches were a part of every trip to his offices in Paris and London. Extended stays in Germany to Baden-Baden, Wiesbaden, the Rhine River Valley, Frankfurt, Heidelberg and Carlsbad involved "health treatments" at the spas. He enjoyed England and Scotland as well as France and Switzerland and traveled to the Holy Lands, Turkey, Italy, North Africa, India, Japan and Alaska.

Despite his personal prestige and fame as a business pioneer, Postmaster General, and Christian statesman, he never lost a child's delight and amazement when in the presence of royalty like Queen Victoria, King Edward VII, King George V and Queen Mary.

His five-week trip with President Benjamin Harrison across the United States in 1891 covered 9,000 miles, in which he viewed America and its people with fascination and interest.

Nothing, however, quite equaled his brief but restful excursions to the New Jersey coastline. In 1872 he and several other friends purchased land at the southernmost tip of the state for the West Cape May Land Company to establish Seagrove, a resort for Presbyterians, called a seaside paradise. Nearby his three-story "cottage," surrounded by verandas on two levels, was the Beadle Memorial Presbyterian Church that he built in 1882 in honor of Rev. Elias Beadle, minister of the Second Presbyterian Church in Philadelphia. So enjoyable were his visits to this area, known today as Cape May Point, that he persuaded President Harrison to visit and Mrs. Harrison to accept, in 1890, the gift of a cottage presented by Wanamaker and friends.

Often staying in Atlantic City, another favorite vacation site for both Wanamaker and his wife, he would slip away on an afternoon train trip to the Cape via Mays Landing, the only route in the days before bridges crossed the bay.

Other vacation places the Wanamakers enjoyed, such as Palm Beach, Florida; Hot Springs, Va.; Sugar Hill, N. H.; Bedford Springs, Pa.; and Saratoga, N.Y. are far to numerous to list.

But being home at Lindenhurst, his manicured 108-acre estate in Jenkintown, brought a special delight and joy to him even when the rest of the family was away. Surrounded by cooks, housekeepers, caretakers and his personal manservant, he was free to read, write, observe and think. Idleness was repulsive to him, but the freedom from the daily demands of home, business and church was its own reward.

Life Meets Death

WITH A ROBUST AND VIGOROUS ATTITUDE THROUGHOUT LIFE, John Wanamaker never planned to die. He never denied its reality, but like Robert Frost, he could only see the many "miles to go before we sleep."

As his son Rodman increasingly shouldered the heavy responsibilities for the daily operation of the business in both cities, the father had more time for longer vacations and was able to devote himself to his broad interests in church and community affairs. His correspondence and appointment calendars, nevertheless, indicate that he was still actively engaged in some routine business decisions as well as in all of the major ones. Retirement never crossed his mind.

Well into his eighties, he kept a most remarkable schedule. He devoted every other day to the store in New York while keeping his main office in Philadelphia. As master of his business he regularly walked through his two stores, greeting customers, conversing with his employees, checking stocks, and looking for ways to improve the business. But the burden of traveling by train and ferryboat between the two cities was bound to take its toll. Unwilling to restrict himself to scheduled office appointments, he would suggest to those who wanted to see him that they simply go to his office in either city and he would find time to meet them without too much delay. He seemed to find time for everyone.

Occasionally he would respond to a letter-writer who was asking for an appointment, by saying,

> As I am so overpressed with work, I ask that you will put in writing the object of your interview and I can make reply to it.[1]

To another, he would actually encourage the individual to visit him, even if he didn't know the person.

Some day when you are near my office, look in and give
me the opportunity of shaking hands and thanking you personally for your letter.[2]

In the last year of his life, he continued to serve as a member of the
Philadelphia Board of Education, President of the Board of Trustees of
Pennsylvania Military College, President of the Pennsylvania State and
World Sunday School Associations, Vice Moderator of the Philadelphia
Presbytery and President of the Huguenot Society. And of course, there
were other organizations like the Masonic Order where he continued as
chairman of the Library Committee. As an early promoter of the 1926
United States Sesqui-Centennial Exposition, which he wanted to be held
in Philadelphia, he met with city, state and national leaders spearheading a
drive to make the event an international effort for peace.

Bethany was always on his mind. Writing to the choir director, he
worried about the decreasing attendance of the choir members from nearly 100 to about 45, and suggested that the names of the absentees be
given to him each week in order that he might contact them personally.

His interest in the Salvation Army never diminished. Concerned
about its leadership he wrote to Commander Evangeline Booth to remain
at the helm as long as she was physically able. Previously supporting the
Colored Y.M.C.A. in Philadelphia, he promised another $20,000 to the
Colored Women's Branch for a dormitory to be named in honor of "my
blind sister, a Christian woman...as a memorial of her life in the simple and
humble way."

He issued another invitation to the Philadelphia Presbytery to hold
their October meeting at Lindenhurst, his country home, where he said
he would entertain them on the grounds after the business sessions, provide dinner for them before they left for home and address them on
"Reminiscences of Presbyterianism in Philadelphia." Then he said, "I shall
go South late in December or the beginning of January when the fierce
weather comes to Philadelphia." He was not going to let up.

The events leading up to his death reveal his determination to use
every ounce of strength possible to fulfill the responsibilities entrusted to
him, regardless of his advanced age.

September 17, 1922 was a busy Sunday at Bethany where he regularly was involved with morning, afternoon and evening meetings.
Monday morning found him at his Philadelphia office, after which he
presided at the regular monthly meeting of the Presbytery. Rising early, at

5 a.m. on Tuesday, he caught the 7 a.m. train to his New York store but returned to Philadelphia early enough to officiate as Vice-Moderator at the installation of a new pastor at the Grace Presbyterian Church at Twenty-second and Federal Streets in Philadelphia.

The next day, fatigue seemed to catch up to him, leaving him with a cold and considerable coughing throughout the day and night that followed. He insisted on going to his office on Thursday, September 21, and was finally persuaded by his physician to leave in the afternoon and return home for some rest. That was his last day in the office. He never returned.

Confined for several weeks at Lindenhurst without much improvement, he was taken to his city home on Walnut Street where on December 12, 1922 he died. Though immediate reports stated that his coughing had led to heart failure, his physician later concluded, in court, that the heart was strong; he had choked to death on dried mucous.

The report of his death was front-page news not only for the Philadelphia papers but also for the *New York Times*. Letters and telegrams of tribute and condolence poured in from President Harding, Governor Sproul, many national leaders, businessmen, politicians, clergymen and citizens everywhere. Bethany Presbyterian Church, at Twenty-second and Bainbridge Streets, prepared for the funeral that taxed the seating capacity of the church.

When news of Wanamaker's death reached City Hall, Mayor J. Hampton Moore immediately ordered all municipal flags to be lowered to half staff, including those at police and fire stations, "to honor the city's first citizen." Governor Sproul in his tribute stated: "Mr. Wanamaker was the most outstanding citizen of Philadelphia. He was more widely known nationally and internationally than any citizen of our day."

Cardinal Dougherty said, "His death is a personal grief to me." The Philadelphia *Evening Bulletin* eulogized him by stating:

> His life is his lasting memorial....As an exemplar of the product of Americanism in its best estate, of the opportunity that our democracy offers, of the unlimited resource of our institutions, this God-fearing citizen lives, though he be dead.[3]

On Thursday, December 14, the day of his funeral, all public schools were ordered closed, City Council and the courts adjourned early and scores of businessmen closed their shops and stores. Other corporations,

*Wanamaker Bell tower mausoleum, St. James the Less Episcopal Church cemetery,
Hunting Park Avenue, Philadelphia*

factories and even movie theaters suspended all business for several minutes at 2:00 p.m., the time of the funeral.

From 9:00 a.m. to noon, two long lines of people entered the church and passed the glass-covered half-opened bronze and silver casket, partially draped with an American flag. Despite a heavy snowfall and an extremely cold wind, 15,000 mourners paid their tribute to their departed friend. "It is the greatest crowd I have ever seen at the funeral of a Philadelphian," commented the police captain in charge.

The majority of the mourners stood outside the church, having been unable to obtain one of the 2400 tickets issued to church members, employees, special friends, and dignitaries.

The brief and simple twenty-five minute service included music by a choir of 125 women all dressed in white, Scripture readings, congregational hymns and a eulogy by the pastor of Bethany.

Among the honorary pall-bearers were Senators George Wharton Pepper and David Reed, Governor William Sproul, Governor-elect Gifford Pinchot, the mayors of Philadelphia and New York, Nathan Strauss, Congressman George Graham, Bishop Joseph Berry, Rabbi Joseph Krauskopf, Cardinal Dougherty, E.T.Stotesbury, Hugh Black, Governor Nathan Miller of New York, William L. McLean, Cyrus H.K.Curtis, Chief Justice William Taft, William Jennings Bryan and Thomas A. Edison.

Special permission granted by the Fairmount Park Commission allowed the funeral cortege to go through the Park to the churchyard of St. James-the-Less Episcopal Church at Thirty-third Street and Hunting Park Avenue in North Philadelphia. Wanamaker's body was then laid at rest in a large, stone, bell-tower mausoleum which had been built by his son Rodman for the burial of his brother Thomas in 1908. There, too, lie the bodies of his wife, Mary Wanamaker, their six children and several other family members. Characteristically, the Wanamaker name is not found on the exterior of the monument. But the message of life and hope, that he taught so faithfully at Bethany for more than sixty years, sounds forth from the music of the bells heard several times each day.

What Was He Really Like?

THE PHOTOGRAPHS OF JOHN WANAMAKER—two-dimensional at best—fail to tell us all we want to know about his physical appearance. Recently discovered among his papers, however, was his passport #13424 issued in Washington, D.C. on June 30, 1871, which gives the following vivid description:

> 34 years, 5 feet 10 inches tall, high forehead, hair—brown, complexion—light, face—oval, eyes—blue, nose—prominent, mouth—small, chin—small. [1]

Photographs reveal that as Wanamaker's years increased, so did his weight, but never to the point that he appeared overweight. He wore glasses but only while reading and seemed to dislike appearing in public with them. Although he never seemed to possess a full head of hair except in his youth, he never became bald. He was always clean shaven and never grew a mustache or beard—uncommon in his day.

It may have been the custom of the day to dress formally, but John Wanamaker *always* wore a coat, vest and bow-tie. On a very hot summer day at Pass-a-Grille, Florida, he wrote to his wife from his second floor room, saying:

> It is now very hot here and I shall now take my coat off as I am all alone. [2]

With his pleasant disposition and optimistic outlook, Wanamaker had a winsome personality that caused most people to like him even if they didn't always agree with him. Even political opponents—with few exceptions—respected him for his integrity, zeal and unquestionable love for God and nation. Few people have had such wide-spread admiration and praise as he received from business leaders, government officials, politicians, educators, clergy of all faiths, employees and the general public.

The Wanamaker Statue

A Celebration Worth Remembering

FEW MEN OR WOMEN ARE MEMORIALIZED with a statue erected in their honor, but John Wanamaker was one of the few.

John Wanamaker, a life-long citizen of Philadelphia, had created a new era in retail merchandising with his one-price system, guaranteed merchandise and the return of goods for any reason. His name had become a household word, and he a friend to multitudes.

When the Founder of the department stores died in 1922 at the age of eighty-four, Philadelphia Mayor J. Hampton Moore immediately proposed that contributions be collected for a statue to honor the man whom he called "the world's most distinguished Merchant."

John T. Windrim, architect, was appointed chairman of the committee to raise funds, select the sculptor and arrange for the erection of the statue. Jules Mastbaum, John Windrim and John Greenwell were among the first donors.

More than 400,000 people contributed over $35,000, which exceeded the cost of the statue. During "Wanamaker Week," which was observed in Philadelphia public schools early in the spring, thousands of school children also gave their pennies, nickels and dimes.

At noon on Thursday, November 29, 1923, upwards of 10,000 people gathered on the east side of City Hall with the Mayor and other city dignitaries. The Police Band of Philadelphia led by Leopold Stokowski, conductor of the Philadelphia Orchestra, provided music. Several hundred cadets of the John Wanamaker Commercial Institute, dressed in their colorful red, white and blue uniforms, stood by in awe and reverence for the man who had given them a free education and a good job.

While Mayor Moore presided at the unveiling ceremonies, former Governor of Pennsylvania, Edwin S. Stuart read a letter from President Warren G. Harding:

John Wanamaker statue, City Hall Plaza, Philadelphia

Mr. Wanamaker was, in many fields of activities, among the most useful Americans of his time, and whatever is calculated to keep alive the inspiration of his career and to impress it upon future generations is certain to be a true public service. [1]

A letter from former President Calvin Coolidge was read before the address by U.S. Senator George Wharton Pepper. Reviewing the life of Wanamaker, Pepper declared:

It is not worthwhile for the speaker on an occasion like this to urge his hearers to follow the example of such a distinguished citizen in whose honor we are here assembled. Such a man's life speaks for itself. His record makes its own appeal. If he struggled for his education, if he began his fight without much backing, if he overcame countless obstacles of all sorts, if he attained high places and if success did not spoil him, the mere record of these facts is more eloquent than a speaker's exhortation. [2]

In his closing comments Pepper spoke of Wanamaker's secure position in the hearts of Philadelphians and said:

As we go homeward, let us remember that it is Thanksgiving Day and that among the many things we have to be thankful for are these three things: that this man lived, that we knew him, and that this enduring monument will perpetuate his memory for the upbuilding and enrichment of Philadelphia. [3]

The statue was unveiled by a fourteen year-old boy scout representing the children and youth of the city.

SCULPTOR— J. MASSEY RHIND
STATUE IN BRONZE—8'6"
WEIGHT OF STATUE—13 TONS
MARBLE / GRANITE PEDESTAL RESTING ON A 4' HIGH CONCRETE SLAB
COST - $21,500

Funds that were donated exceeded the cost of the statue by $14,079.75. The sum of $10,000 was given to the Presbyterian Hospital for "The John Wanamaker Memorial Room." An additional $3,000 was placed in trust for the perpetual care and cleaning of the statue and for the placing of a wreath on Wanamaker's birthday (July 11). The remainder was used for publication of a memorial booklet.

A copper box measuring twelve inches square and deep, and hermetically sealed, was placed in the foundation of the statue. It contains a copy of President Harding's letter endorsing the movement to erect the statue, a photograph of Mayor Moore, a copy of J. W. Riley's poem, "The Inner Side of Every Cloud," a white aster, copies of Philadelphia newspapers, invitations to the unveiling, Philadelphia City Council minutes and an impression in gold of the seal of the city. [4]

The U.S. Sesqui-Centennial and the Wanamaker Bell

FAR ABOVE MARKET STREET IN PHILADELPHIA, just a stone's throw from City Hall, hangs the massive 15 1/2-ton Wanamaker Bell modestly referred to by its donor as "The Founder's Bell." Rodman Wanamaker gave Philadelphia a memorial to his father and, unsuspectingly, to himself, the fame of which could outlast the fame of their mercantile enterprise.

Inspired by the sound of London's "Big Ben" one sleepless night, the son of John Wanamaker conceived the idea of placing a bell atop his Philadelphia store as a tribute to his father and to the founders of America whether in politics, business, education, industry, medicine or other professions. With patriotic zeal he planned the presentation of this bell to occur on July 4, 1926, the Sesqui-Centennial of the United States, as part of the festivities in Philadelphia, the birthplace of the nation.

John Wanamaker had been one of the primary promoters of the Sesqui-Centennial celebration, using his influence to convince President Harding of the international significance of such an event. In 1921 he wrote to the President:

> The Great Exhibition of Great Britain was held at Hyde Park, London from May 1 to Oct. 5, 1851. Prince Albert, the consort of Queen Victoria was at the head of it and active in promoting its success.
>
> The Centennial Exhibition was held in Fairmount Park, Philadelphia, from May 10 to Oct. 10, 1876, and so far as known surpassed any exhibition ever held.
>
> Forty five years have rolled by since 1876, and 1926 will complete another half-century. To many it seems eminently proper to celebrate a Sesqui-Centennial not only to

take note of the progress of the United States but to bring together all the nations of the world into peaceful competition for supremacy and mutual brotherhood. [1]

In 1921, Philadelphia Mayor J. Hampton Moore, appointed a Board of Directors for the Sesqui-Centennial celebration. The Board then elected John Wanamaker as chairman of a committee to visit the President and members of Congress for their approval and financial support. Laboring vigorously, despite the opposition of indifference, Wanamaker succeeded in his efforts and was unquestionably the unsung hero in bringing about the celebration, although he did not live to see it.

For 187 days, from June 1 to December 1, 1926, Philadelphia was the focus of the nation. More than five million visitors passed under a colossal eighty-foot replica of the Liberty Bell, adorned with 26,000 fifteen-watt bulbs, which spanned South Broad Street at Oregon Avenue, the entrance to the Sesqui-Centennial grounds at League Island Park.

The Wanamaker's "Founder's Bell" in transit to Philadelphia from the New York harbor, 1926

Almost 1000 acres of land adjoining the U.S. Naval Yard were utilized for the exhibit buildings, the Gladway Amusement Center, parking areas and a military encampment.

Directly inside the main entrance was an immense auditorium with seating capacity for 15,000, a center for various musical and dramatic events. In addition, an enormous open-air stadium seating 100,000 was built for patriotic pagents and sports events and became famous for the Tunney-Dempsey fight. [In later years it hosted the annual Army and Navy Football Classic and was renamed the John F. Kennedy Stadium in honor of the assassinated president.] Also completed in time for the festivities was the Delaware River Bridge, the first vehicular bridge between Philadelphia and Camden, New Jersey. [It was later renamed the Benjamin Franklin Bridge.]

Various States of the Union and more than two dozen foreign countries created exhibits for the Sesqui-Centennial. Among them stood the Palace of Liberal Arts which housed numerous displays and exhibits. Here the Hall of Flags displayed a remarkable array of American flags "from the time of Columbus until now." The exhibit contained a small portion of the international flag collection of Rodman Wanamaker, begun in 1903 and numbering almost 3500 flags.

The single room exhibit, designed in colonial style architecture, also displayed various paintings of American history, a chair reportedly used at the signing of the "Declaration of Independence" and a swatch of the original bunting used by Betsy Ross in making the first American flag adopted by Congress. This was a gift from Anne Balderston, a direct descendent of Betsy Ross. Across the entrance to the display was the name of John Wanamaker—a not-so-subtle publicity scheme to be sure—but also a reminder of Wanamaker's unquestionable patriotic love for flag and country.

THE FOUNDERS BELL

Not content with a flag display that would be forgotten when the exhibition closed, Rodman concentrated on the Founder's Bell for many months. With determination that it be one of the world's finest and largest bells, he dispatched Mary Vogt, the noted store organist, on an extensive research tour to ascertain the qualities and virtues of famous bells throughout Europe. Some years later she wrote:

> Bells are very human things, they almost breathe they are so sensitive. Remember the little Chinese story which depicted the little Chinese girl being thrown into the metal to provide a beautiful tone? [2]

Reviewing a very detailed comparison of size, tone and operation of those bells, Rodman selected Gillett & Johnston (The Croyden Bell Foundry, Ltd.) of Croyden, England to cast a bell weighing approximately 15 tons.

Throughout the winter and spring, Rodman was almost beside himself with anxiety to be sure that the bell would be in place by July 4. In a letter dated February 1, 1926, he wrote:

> We want no tower of any kind for the present. No swinging bell, simply a bracing of steel, safe enough to hold the bell even if it is only 5 feet from the top of the tower. We care nothing for the various arguments advanced by any-one....Simply ring the bell July 4, 1926. The rest I must be responsible for later on. Just hang the bell, even if only on bricks or the iron beams that will make it safe. [3]

But correspondence reveals that when the huge bell was first cast, a defect in it necessitated a melt-down and its recasting, which unfortunately delayed its completion. The recasting proceeded with a new bell that weighed a little over 15 1/2 tons. The total weight of bell, headstock and clapper was 17 1/4 tons.

Hoping that the bell would be completed by July, Rodman arranged for the fastest shipping available and for a temporary housing structure for the bell on the rooftop of the store—anything that would allow the bell to be rung on the Fourth. But the job just could not be done in time. Though Rodman was accustomed to having things done when and where he wanted no matter what the cost, money was not the problem here. The problem was time and perfection.

When the bell was not completed for the July celebration, Rodman was insistent that it be put in place before the Sesqui-Centennial year ended. The last day of December [New Year's Eve] was chosen for the bell's inauguration. It would be a fitting close of the year-long celebration ringing out the old year and ringing in the new.

The bell arrived by ship in New York Harbor where store officials and cadets of the John Wanamaker Commercial Institute were on hand and then was transported by barge to New Jersey and by freight train to Philadelphia. The bell's journey was well documented by a photographer.

Crowds gathered on Juniper Street at City Hall on December 23 to watch the bell being hoisted to the steel and brick superstructure towering more than 100 feet above the roof of the Wanamaker store. The newspapers extolled the virtues of the bell, "the largest in the Western Hemisphere" at that time.

The inauguration of the bell was held on December 31, 1926 at 5:30 p.m. in a ceremony led by Rodman Wanamaker in the Grand Court. He declared:

> Ringing from Free America, the Home of the Liberty Bell, the earth and the skies vibrate with the message of The Founder's Bell—a message of Patriotism, of Truth, of Faith, of Love, and of Peace...
>
> The Store Family, as the Founder always called us, pledge ourselves to build with the spirit of our heritage and inspiration—with
>
> the plumb of HONOR
> the level of TRUTH
> and the square of
> INTEGRITY
> EDUCATION
> COURTESY and
> MUTUALITY.

Quoting the credo of his father, Rodman renewed his own commitment to the high ideals and principles of his father and to the nation celebrating its 150th anniversary.

> It is the largest in the Western Hemisphere—9 feet 6 inches in diameter, 7 feet 9 inches in height, weighing 38,640 pounds or 17 & 1/4 long tons.
>
> It is tuned on the five-tone harmonic principle, giving a purity and sonority to its note—low D—unequaled by any bell in the world.

In addition the booklet noted that it was the first bell of its size to be cast and tuned with a 5-tone harmonic vibration. [This means that the bell sounds a complete chord simultaneously, providing a very rich and pure tone.] It cost 6,780 pounds sterling and is believed to be the sixth largest bell in the United States today and is larger than Big Ben.

Though Wanamaker wanted a fixed bell that was "not to swing when in position, but is to be operated in stroke by a hammer, through a clock mechanism," the bell was actually constructed so that it could either be swung or struck by a hammer. Due to excessive vibrations when the bell was swung and rung by its 11'10" long clapper and 3'7" round ball, the bell has remained immobile in recent years and is struck by a 500-pound hammer.

In addition to the Founder's Credo and signature, the Bell also carries the following inscription:

JULY 4 1926

ONE HUNDRED FIFTY YEARS

AMERICAN INDEPENDENCE

1776 - 1926

FIFTY YEARS

MERCANTILE INDEPENDENCE

THE NEW KIND OF STORE

1876 - 1926

A SEQUEL

WHEN WANAMAKER'S BUILT the twenty-seven-story Lincoln-Liberty Building in the adjoining block at Broad and Chestnut Streets in 1932 to house their expanding Men's Store, the Bell was moved to a new location on its roof. It rests in a specially designed super-structure 474 feet above the sidewalk and can be easily seen from many downtown streets. The Bell strikes each quarter hour from 9 a.m. to 9 p.m.—except Sundays and holidays—with the hour of twelve taking two and one-half minutes to ring.

In 1952 the Lincoln-Liberty Building with the Bell was sold to The Philadelphia National Bank, presently owned by CoreStates Financial Corp. The building is identified throughout various parts of the city by the sixteen foot high letters "PNB" on all four sides of the super-structure, just above the Bell.

The Founder's Bell being raised to the tower of the Lincoln-Liberty Building, Broad and Chestnut Streets, Philadelphia, 1931

From Then 'til Now

THE INTENT OF THIS BOOK has been to retell the fascinating story of one man whose life was devoted to others through his business, religious, political and civic involvements. One small volume can do little more than briefly touch upon the numerous facets of his life. Unlike some great individuals who became known for their success or contribution to a single profession or endeavor, John Wanamaker's life involved several areas during more than eight decades.

Some readers will note obvious omissions in the story while others may wish for a different interpretation of the facts. Later publications and other writers will undoubtedly serve that purpose. This writer, however, in this small capsule, has sought to highlight not only John Wanamaker's achievements but also his unrelenting determination and perseverance in bridging the gap that so often exists between the secular marketplace and the sacred house of worship. As a man of consistency, it mattered not to him where he was; the basic life principles of decency, honesty, fairness, and consideration for others had to be upheld, whatever the cost.

The book ends with the death of Rodman Wanamaker in 1928 though there is so much to tell of the events since then. That also will have to be left to others, except for the following brief update.

Louis Rodman Wanamaker, the greatly loved and well-trained son, became the sole owner of the two John Wanamaker stores in Philadelphia and New York following the death of his father. He died just six years later in 1928 at the age of sixty-five. Records show that he perpetuated the same philosophy of business as his father and actually saw sales increase in his lone years. Whereas the Founder had given his son Rodman a free rein to run the business, Rodman's will placed daily operations in the hands of "professional managers" and out of direct family stewardship.

Father and son were both spared the devastating experiences of the Great Depression and the declining effect upon businesses across the nation. Further problems developed during World War II at which time the trustees of the Rodman Wanamaker estate managed the business on behalf of the family.

In the post-war expansion period, Wanamakers, like many other "downtown businesses" began to branch out with new stores in Wilmington, Del., Westchester, N.Y., Wynnewood, Pa., Jenkintown, Pa., King of Prussia, Pa., Moorestown, N.J., and several other areas. By 1978 there were sixteen stores, including the flag-ship at Thirteenth and Market Streets in Philadelphia and others as far away as Reading, Pa., Harrisburg, Pa., Scranton, Pa., and Westchester, N.Y. The profit margin, however, was not satisfactory and it was time to make a major move.

Carter, Hawley, Hale, a major retailer based in Los Angeles operating seventy-two full-line department stores, thirty-one high fashion specialty stores and several other subsidiaries, purchased the sixteen John Wanamaker stores in 1978, promising to raise the chain to previously unequaled heights. It was an ambitious goal, easier to put on paper than to bring to reality.

Subsequently, John Wanamaker was sold in 1986 to Detroit real estate developer A. Alfred Taubman. Operationally, the store was merged with Woodward and Lothrop of Washington, D.C. Buying, credit and operations were relocated to Virginia.

The Philadelphia flag-ship store has now down-sized to five floors and restored the once-famed beauty of the Grand Court and its surroundings, long in need of repair. A major investment has been made by Taubman to upgrade the Great Organ with the latest state-of-the-art technology, soon to be completed. But even during the reconstruction, customers and friends still enjoy the music of the world's largest organ, played twice daily in free public concert in the store.

Prior to this renovation, this center-city Historic Landmark building was sold to John Kasmirsky of California and is now managed by Brickstone Realty. The John Wanamaker store occupies the first five floors of the building. The upper seven floors comprise an office building with a separate Juniper Street entrance and an underground three-level garage accommodating 660 cars. The new four-story atrium on the ninth floor also serves as the beautiful entrance-way to the famous Crystal Tea Room, one of Philadelphia's largest and most popular restaurants since its opening in 1911. Soon it, too, will be re-opened to the public.

Presently, fourteen other branch stores [one was sold] bearing the signature of John Wanamaker, one of America's greatest merchants, endeavor to provide the service and uphold the hard-earned and well-deserved reputation of the Founder.

Recently Mr. Arnold Aronson, Chairman and Chief Executive Officer of Woodward and Lothrop, John Wanamaker, wrote to this writer about John Wanamaker and said:

> His business and personal ethic is an inspiration to those of us who have inherited his great franchise and in whose name we strive to maintain and update this retail institution.[1]

This book has been written for all those who find inspiration in the lives of others whose self-confidence, self-sacrifice, tenacity and courage have not been daunted by adversity or rejection. May it make the reader proud to be a part of a world that produces a man like John Wanamaker.

John Wanamaker, 1921

ENDNOTES

With exceptions as noted, all unpublished letters and speeches as well as many other pamphlets, booklets and documents listed below are part of the John Wanamaker Collection at the Historical Society of Pennsylvania, Philadelphia, Pa. They have been used by permission of the Society and denoted, HSP.

A Young Lad Keeps His Vow
> p.1,   #1   *The Golden Book of the Wanamaker Stores* (Philadelphia, 1911), p.135.

A Child Is Born
> p.7,   #1   Herbert Adams Gibbons, *John Wanamaker* (New York and London: Harper & Brothers Publishers, 1926), vol.1, p.37.

Y.M.C.A.
> p.11,   #1   Unpublished letter of John R. Mott, June 21, 1924. HSP.
> p.12,   #2   Unpublished letter of John Wanamaker, December 10, 1900. HSP.

Genesis
> p.22,   #1   "30th Anniversary, March 1906," p.35. HSP.
> p.24,   #2   *Philadelphia Sunday Gazette*, April 8, 1877.
>   #3   *Sunday Mercury*, quoted in *The Golden Book of the Wanamaker Stores*, p.61.
>   #4   *Public Ledger*, July 28, 1897, p.11.
>   #5   "Annals of the Wanamaker System," 1896. p.5. HSP.
> p.29,   #6   Elbert Hubbard, "Pastelles in Prose: A Visit to John Wanamaker New York and Philadelphia," 1907. HSP.
> p.30,   #7   Unpublished letter of Thomas B. Wanamaker, December 17, 1907. HSP.
> p.31,   #8   Unpublished letter of Thomas B. Wanamaker, December 20, 1907. HSP.
>   #9   Joseph H. Appel, *The Business Biography of John Wanamaker, Founder and Builder* (New York: The Macmillan Company, 1930), p.147.
> p.32,   #10   John Wanamaker's personal diary, November 1907. HSP.
> p.33,   #11   *The Golden Book*, p.1.
> p.35,   #12   "America the Beautiful," Katherine Lee Bates.
> p.36,   #13   Appel, *The Business Biography*, p.196.
>   #14   *The Golden Book*, vol. 2, 1913, p.3.

An Advertising Genius
> p.39,   #1   Unpublished "Record of a personal interview with John Wanamaker by Frank G. Carpenter," 1897, p.4. HSP.
> p.40,   #2   Gibbons, *John Wanamaker*, vol. 2, p.19.

p.41, #3 Appel, *The Business Biography of John Wanamaker*, p.389.
#4 *Ibid.*, p.398.
#5 Unpublished letter of John Wanamaker, n.d. HSP.
#6 *Philadelphia Record*, February 10, 1890, p.5.
p.42, #7 "30th Anniversary, March 1906," p.48. HSP.
#8 "Ceremony of Dedication of the New House of Business," 1911. HSP.
p.43, #9 "Wanamaker's Grand Depot," 1878. HSP.
p.44, #10 Copy of an unpublished letter of John Wanamaker to General Thomas J. Stewart, Friendly Sons of St. Patrick, March 17, 1906. HSP.
#11 *The Golden Book*, p.224.

Tell It Like It Is!
p.45, #1 "The Printers Ink," undated news clipping. HSP.

The Great Organ
p.47, #1 "The Great Organ," John Wanamaker, p.5, nd.

Munkacsy Paintings
p.50, #1 *Christ Before Pilate*, Published by C.H.Sedelmeyer, 1888. HSP.

Eagle
p.52, #1 "Descriptive Catalog of the German Arts and Crafts at the Universal Exposition, St. Louis, 1904," Published by the Imperial German Commission. HSP.

John Wanamaker Commercial Institute
p.56, #1 Unpublished letter of John Wanamaker, August 14, 1913. HSP.
p.57, #2 Unpublished letter of John Wanamaker to Governor Hastings, April 23, 1898. HSP.
#3 Unpublished letter of Captain John Wanamaker, n.d. HSP.
p.58, #4 "Handbook of the John Wanamaker Commercial Institute." HSP.
p.59, #5 Appel, *The Business Biography*, New York: The MacMillan Co. 1930), p.430.
p.60, #6 Unpublished speech of John Wanamaker, n.d. HSP.

A Pioneer in Business
p.61, #1 Tennyson, Alfred Lord, "Ulysses."

A Young Man Turns to God
p.65, #1 Unpublished letter of John Wanamaker, May 26, 1917. HSP.

Bethany
p.66, #1 Unpublished speech of John Wanamaker, 1889. HSP.
p.68, #2 Appel, *The Business Biography*, pp. 34-35.
p.69, #3 Unpublished speech of John Wanamaker, April 26, 1921. HSP.

p.70, #4 "History of the First Independent Church of Philadelphia," November 24, 1859. p.52. HSP.

p.71, #5 Unpublished Diary of John Wanamaker, January 1, 1860. HSP.

p.73, #6 "1904-1905 Manual and Directory," Men's Brotherhood, p.24. HSP.

#7 "Bethany Collegiate Presbyterian Church Yearbook 1914," p. 17. HSP.

p.74, #8 Gibbons, *John Wanamaker*, vol. 2, p.38.

#9 "1904-05 Manual and Directory," Men's Brotherhood. p.19.

p.75, #10 Unpublished letter of John Wanamaker, n.d., HSP.

p.76, #11 "Bethany Collegiate Presbyterian Yearbook 1914," p. 21. HSP.

#12 A. Gordon Mac Lennan, *Prayers of John Wanamaker* (New York: Fleming H. Revell Co., 1927), p.18.

p.79, #13 A. Gordon Mac Lennan, *Prayers at Bethany Chapel by John Wanamaker* (New York: Fleming H. Revell Co., 1925), p.31.

#14 Mac Lennan, *Prayers of John Wanamaker*, p.35.

p.80, #15 *Philadelphia Record*, February 10, 1890, p.1.

#16 Unpublished letter of John Wanamaker, March 12, 1888. Author's collection.

#17 Unpublished speech of John Wanamaker, December 1918. HSP.

p.81, #18 Gibbons, *John Wanamaker*, vol. 1, p.51.

#19 Russell H. Conwell, *The Romantic Rise of a Great American* (New York and London: Harper & Brothers, 1924), p.136.

p.84, #20 "Silver Anniversary of Bethany Temple Presbyterian Church, 1931," p. 24. Author's collection.

p.87, #21 Unpublished letter of John Wanamaker to the Abington Presbyterian Church, September 4, 1872. HSP.

p.88, #22 Unpublished letter of John Wanamaker, October, 1898. HSP.

Pious John

p.90, #1 Appel, *The Business Biography*, p.25.

#2 Mac Lennan, *Prayers of John Wanamaker*, p.47.

p.91, #3 John Wanamaker's personal diary, Oct.1899. HSP.

p.94, #4 *The Speeches of Hon. John Wanamaker on Quayism and Boss Domination in Pennsylvania Politics.* (Business Men's Republican League of the State of Pennsylvania, The Bourse) Philadelphia, Pa., 1898, p.55. HSP.

#5 "Christmas Carols," John Wanamaker, Philadelphia, Pa., n.d. Author's collection.

p.96, #6 *John Wanamaker Leads in Prayer* (New York and Newark, New Jersey: Barse & Hopkins, 1921), pp.26-27.

#7 "Lead Kindly Light," John Henry Newman, 1801-1890.

#8 Unpublished letter of John Wanamaker, February 25, 1898. HSP.

33rd Degree Mason

p.99, #1 "Odd Fellows Siftings," September 1911. HSP.

#2 Unpublished letter of John Wanamaker, July 30, 1917. HSP.

Postmaster

  p.104, #1 *Annual Report of the Postmaster General of the United States for the fiscal year ending June 30, 1889.* Government Printing Office, Washington, D.C., p.3.

  p.106, #2 *Annual Report of the Postmaster General of the United States for the fiscal year ending June 30, 1891.*,Government Printing Office, Washington, D.C., p. 48.

  p.108, #3 "Postal Savings System Report," Office of the Postmaster General. August 1988.

  p.109, #4 Letter from Mr. Herb Collins to author, October, 1992.

  p.110, #5 *Annual Report of the Postmaster General of the United States for the fiscal year ending June 30, 1892,* Government Printing Office. Washington, D.C., p.910.

  p.111, #6 *Ibid.,* p. 910.

  p.113, #7 *Ibid.,* p.3.

Politics

  p.114, #1 Gibbons, *John Wanamaker,* vol. 1. p.345.

  p.115, #2 James A. Kehl, *Boss Rule in the Golden Age.* (Pittsburgh, Pa.: University of Pittsburgh Press, 1981).

  p.118, #3 *The Speeches of Hon. John Wanamaker on Quayism and Boss Domination in Pennsylvania Politics.* p.163.

  p.120, #4 *Ibid.,* p.12.

     #5 *Ibid.,* p.15.

  p.121, #6 *Ibid.,* pp.178-183.

     #7 *Ibid.,* p.25.

  p.122, #8 *Ibid.,* p.7.

Writer

  p.125, #1 *Everybody's Journal,* vol. 6, no. 4, Philadelphia, Pa.,1876. HSP.

  p.126, #2 *The Farm Journal,* vol. 1, no. 9, Philadelphia, November 1877.

  p.127, #3 Gibbons, *John Wanamaker,* vol 1, pp.198-199.

     #4 *Farm Journal,* vol. 1. no.1, Philadelphia, March 1877, p.1.

  p.131, #5 Unpublished letter of John Wanamaker, June 23, 1887. HSP.

  p.132, #6 Bookplate in Nathaniel Hawthorne's, *Twice Told Tales,* (Philadelphia: Henry Altemus), n.d. Author's collection.

  p.133, #7 *The Ladies' Journal,* September 1879. HSP.

Editorials of John Wanamaker

  p.136, #1 Appel, *The Business Biography,* p.222.

  p.138 #2 Wanamaker Collection. HSP.

Letter to a Friend in Sorrow

  p.153, #1 Unpublished letter of John Wanamaker, November 30, 1910. Author's collection.

What Was He Really Like?
        p.206, #1 United States Passport of John Wanamaker, issued June 30, 1871, #13424. HSP.

               #2 Unpublished letter of John Wanamaker, February 28, 1917. HSP.

Statue
        p.209, #1 "Dedication of the Memorial Statue of John Wanamaker." November, 1923, p.9. HSP.

               #2 *Ibid.*, p.7.

               #3 *Ibid.*, p.8.

        p.210, #4 *Evening Bulletin,* Novermber 27, 1923.

The Wanamaker Bell
        p.212, #1 Original unpublished handwritten letter of John Wanamaker, 1921. HSP.

        p.214, #2 Copy of unpublished letter of Mary Vogt, n.d. HSP.

               #3 Unpublished letter of Rodman Wanamaker, February 1, 1926. HSP.

From Then 'til Now
        p.220, #1 Unpublished letter of Arnold H. Aronson, June 17, 1991. Author's collection. Used by Permission.

BIBLIOGRAPHY

This writer has had the unique advantage of uninhibited access to the personal correspondence, records and files of John Wanamaker dating from 1858 to his death in 1922. Correspondence and records of his son Rodman and of the John Wanamaker stores until 1986 have also been reviewed in detail.

A most remarkable source of original material—including hundreds of booklets, pamphlets, catalogs and articles about Wanamaker—has been carefully studied by courtesy of both the Historical Society of Pennsylvania and the Bethany Collegiate Presbyterian Church. Fifteen-thousand carefully indexed research cards of Herbert Adams Gibbons, Wanamaker's biographer of 1926, have been used extensively in addition to several thousand cards and two dozen loose-leaf notebooks containing information acquired and documented by the present writer.

It seems unnecessary to list all the individual items found in the Wanamaker files at the Historical Society of Pennsylvania, but the bibliography below will help other researchers.

A Book of Cape May, New Jersey. Cape May, New Jersey: Albert Hand Co., 1937.

Annual Report of the Postmaster General of the United States for the Fiscal Year Ending June 30, 1889. Government Printing Office, Washington, D.C.

Annual Report of the Postmaster General of the United States. June 30, 1891.

Annual Report of the Postmaster General of the United States. June 30, 1892.

Appel, Joseph H. *The Business Biography of John Wanamaker, Founder and Builder.* New York: The MacMillan Co., 1930.

_____. *John Wanamaker: A Study.* Philadelphia, Penna.: The MacMillan Co., 1927.

Archival Materials. (Courtesy of the Historical Society of Pennsylvania, Philadelphia) John Wanamaker's personal and family correspondence, business records, advertising material, trade cards, personal memorabilia, personal dairies and datebooks, publicity releases, store financial records, property deeds, church and political correspondence, scrapbooks, photographs, Mary Wanamaker's letters, and Rodman Wanamaker's letters.

Baltzell, E. Digby. *Philadelphia Gentlemen.* Glencoe, Il.: The Free Press, 1958.

Bethany Collegiate Presbyterian Church Yearbook, 1913.

Burt, Nathaniel. *The Perennial Philadephians.* Boston, Toronto: Little, Brown & Co., 1963.

Burt, Oliver W. *John Wanamaker, Boy Merchant.* The Bobbs-Merrill Co., Inc., 1962

Conwell, Russell H. *The Romantic Rise of A Great American*. New York and London: Harper and Brothers Publishers, 1924.

Cushing, Marshall. *The Story of Our Post Office*. Boston, Mass.: A.M. Thayer & Co., 1893.

Dixon, Joseph K. *The Vanishing Race*. New York: Bonanza, 1913.

Fergus, Charles. *Shadow Catcher*. New York: Soho Press, 1991.

Gibbons, Herbert Adams. *John Wanamaker*. 2 vols. New York and London: Harper and Brothers Publishers, 1926.

Golden Book of the Wanamaker Stores. Philadelphia, 1911.

Hale, Edward Everett, Intro. *Giants of the Republic*. Philadelphia: J.H. Moore Co., 1895.

Hazelhurst, George. *A Part of Old Philadelphia*. Philadelphia, 1913.

Hendrickson, Robert. *The Grand Emporiums*. New York: Stein & Day, 1979.

Hewlett, Joseph Mitchell, Jr. *The Cromley Family (Gramlich) of Philadelphia*. Wyncote, Penna. 1959.

Historical Souvenir, 225th Anniversary of the Founding of Philadelphia. Oct. 1908.

Holbrook, Stewart. *The Age of the Moguls*. Garden City, New York: Doubleday & Co., 1953.

Jackson, Joseph. *America's Most Historic Highway*. Philadelphia, New York: John Wanamaker, 1926.

Jackson, Joseph, ed. *Quaint Corners in Philadelphia*. Philadelphia & New York: John Wanamaker, 1922.

John Wanamaker Leads in Prayer. New York, N.Y. and Newark, N.J.: Barse and Hopkins, 1921.

John Wanamaker: The Record of a Citizen's Celebration to Mark His Sixty Years Career as a Merchant. Philadelphia, 1921.

John Wanamaker's personal diaries.

Kehl, James A. *Boss Rule in the Gilded Age*. Pittsburgh, Pa.: University of Pittsburgh Press, 1981.

King, Moses. *Philadelphia's Most Notable Philadelphians*. Philadelphia, 1902

Krouse, Susan Applegate. "Capturing the Vanishing Race: The Photographs of Dr. Joseph K. Dixon." Master's thesis, Indiana University, 1980.

Lord, John. *Beacon Lights of History*. New York: Clark Co., 1967.

MacLennan, A. Gordon. ed. *Prayers at Bethany Chapel by John Wanamaker*. New York, Chicago, London and Edinburgh: Fleming H. Revell Company, 1925.

_____. *Prayers of John Wanamaker*. New York: Fleming H. Revell Company, 1927.

Maxims of Life and Business by John Wanamaker. Introduction by Russell H. Conwell. New York and London: Harper and Brothers, 1923.

McElroy's Philadelphia City Directory For 1865. Philadelphia: A. McElroy, 1865.

McIntire, Henry B. *Philadelphia Then and Now*. Philadelphia, 1936.

Pictorial Program of the 35th Anniversary of Bethany. Philadelphia, 1893.

"Postal Savings System Report," Office of the Postmaster General. August 1988.

Rigler, Jean Gurney. *Wannemacher/Wanamaker Families of Pennsylvania: A Genealogical Dictionary*. Honolulu, Hawaii: 1984.

Schmertz, Fred., ed. *The Wanamaker Millrose Story: History of the Millrose Athletic Association 1908-1967*. Yonkers, New York.

Smith, Albert Hatcher. *The Life of Russell H. Conwell*. Boston, New York, Chicago: Silver, Burdett & Co., 1899.

Stackpole, E.J. *Behind the Scenes with a Newspaper Man*. Philadelphia & London: J.B. Lippincott Co., 1927.

Stevens, Lewis Townsend. *The History of Cape May County, New Jersey*. Cape May City, New Jersey: Lewis T. Stevens Publisher, 1897.

The Sesqui-centennial International Exposition. Philadelphia: The Women's Committee, 1926.

The Speeches of Hon. John Wanamaker on Quayism and Boss Domination in Pennsylvania Politics. Philadelphia: Business Men's Republican League of the State of Pennsylvania, n.d.

The Wanamaker Diary. Philadelphia: John Wanamaker. series 1902-1961.

U.S. Postal Savings System Report, August 1958.

Wanamaker, John. *Life of Isaiah Williamson.* Reprint. Alumni Association of the Williamson Free School of Mechanical Trades, 1972.

Wanamaker, John. *Prayers of John Wanamaker.* New York, Chicago, London and Edinburgh: Fleming H. Revell Co., 1927.

Wasson, Samuel A. Jr. *History of the Bethany Presbyterian Church and Sunday School 1858-1958.*

White, Wm. P., and Scott, William H. *The Presbyterian Church in Philadelphia.* Philadelphia: Allen, Lane & Scott, 1895.

Whiteman. *Gentlemen in Crises.* Philadelphia: The Union League. n.d.

Wilson, Philip W. *An Unofficial Statesman: Robert C. Ogden.* New York: Doubleday, 1924.

INDEX

William Allen Zulker's multi-faceted career includes thirty years employment in college administration at Eastern College, St. Davids, Pa. He recently retired as Assistant to the President and started working on a Masters of Library Science degree. Also a Presbyterian minister, he is a well-known guest speaker in numerous churches throughout the Philadelphia area.

His interest in John Wanamaker began in the 1950s when he served as minister of the Bethany Temple Presbyterian Church in Philadelphia, one of the four churches founded by Wanamaker. Zulker heard many of his parishioners reflect upon the influence Wanamaker had upon their lives.

When the Wanamaker Collection of more than a million documents was acquired by the Historical Society of Pennsylvania in 1988, Zulker volunteer to assist in processing the papers—a task that continues to this day.

Zulker and his wife are the parents of three daughters and eight grandchildren.